In Silence with God

In Silence with God

by BENEDICT BAUR, O.S.B.
Archabbot of Beuron

translated from the fourth German edition by
Elisabethe Corathiel-Noonan

SCEPTER PUBLISHERS

PRINCETON, NEW JERSEY

Nihil Obstat   Jacob Rea, *Censor deputatus*
Imprimatur   Joseph, *Bishop of the Diocese of Clifton (England)*
                June 28, 1955

First published as *Still mit Gott* (Krefeld-Traar: Verlag St. Andreas, 1951)
English translation published 1955 by Henry Regnery Company

This edition reprinted in 1997 by Scepter Publishers
P.O. Box 1270, Princeton, New Jersey 08542, USA
ISBN 0–933932–93–6

Composition by Shoreline Graphics, Rockland, Maine 04841
Printed in the United States of America

Contents

Introduction

THE VERY title of this book is a challenge. Has there ever been an age more loquacious than ours, one more extroverted, one more concerned with the surface of things? Facing the issue squarely, this book deals with silence, with that inner silence of the soul which the Psalmist has in mind where he says that we should "listen to what the Lord God will say" (Ps 84: 9).

The inner life is the theme of this book. It deals with its very essence. Archabbot Benedict Baur shows the way to his readers on the strength of a life-long experience. As the head of one of the most renowned Benedictine communities of Europe, as an ascetic writer, scholar, and educator, and particularly as a retreat master, he has long won an international following. There could be no safer guide for those who wish to penetrate more deeply into the mysteries of divine revelation, so as to master the confusion of a progress-mad civilization.

Modern man finds it difficult to pursue such a path. Our age is no longer familiar with the language of mystery. Modern man rarely listens to what God has to tell him. He is overwhelmed by a constant stream of words poured out from printing presses and loudspeakers. Most of the outpouring leaves no impact on the minds so widely dulled that independent thinking becomes difficult. The Christians are no exception. They, too, are caught in the noisy stream. They, too, have widely lost the faculty of listening to their inner voice.

St. Paul has said we should not "be conformed to this world" (Rom 12: 2), and he knew what he was talking about, for in his day, just as in our own, people were exposed to influences causing instability and fidgetiness. In his day, too, Christians were traveling on the road of least resistance, adapting themselves to the wavering standards of the majority.

It was because of this very danger that St. Paul wanted them to be "transformed in the newness of their minds, that they might discern what is the good and acceptable and perfect will of God."

To be transformed in such newness, in St. Paul's day as in ours, means *agere contra*, to free oneself of the prevailing trends, to gain a foothold in the realm of the spirit. There is no other remedy in the midst of the distractions and futilities of a mankind bent on seeking salvation by its own efforts, and trying to make the relative values absolute.

More than ever the trend of our age is toward activism. Modern man seems determined to assert himself in building a dream world of his own, divorced from God, and the achievements of technology appear to justify his shallow optimism. Yet, the uneasy feeling underneath, what the French aptly call a *malaise* persists. For modern man is as much, nay, even more lost amidst the world's whirl than man was in St. Paul's times.

The danger signals in many fields of public endeavor are obvious enough to those who have eyes to see. The sober-minded realize that the only antidote is to "cast off," as St. Gregory of Nazianzum says, "the dead works and give place to the Spirit." To help achieve this end is the purpose of this book, which points the way to Christians who are not Christians in name only, to gain a knowledge of their faith that reaches into the depth rather than being confined to the surface.

Those who follow the path Archabbot Benedict Baur indicates will find that they need a new incentive to overcome the mere routine of their religious life. The mainspring of their soul must be wound again. What they have lost by conforming to the world, all too intensely, must be regained by again conforming to the inner voice which they have not harkened to in the midst of an anthill of worldly preoccupations. In again surrendering to the divine, rather than to the natural order, by becoming integrated once more with the sacramental rather than with the profane life, they will attain the inner kingdom of God which means life eternal.

Fundamentally, there is nothing new in Archabbot Baur's approach to the inner life, but he says things long familiar to us by using a language adapted skillfully to our present-day needs. His message is the message of Christ, which he conveys succinctly and in terms so simple and straightforward that the impact becomes unavoidable and yet wholesome to a rare degree.

He but echoes the words of the Psalmist: "Incline my heart, O Lord, unto thy precepts, turn away my eyes that they may not behold vanity, and quicken me in thy way" (Ps 119: 36–37). He wants his readers to realize that they must turn away from, and rise above, the visible sphere of life to gain access to the realities of another world not visible. He wants us to appreciate fully the meaning of Scripture's word that faith is "the evidence of things that are not seen" (Heb 11: 1). In an age when the dominant perspectives are what we might call centrifugal, turned away from the center of creation, away from God, he wants the right order to be restored, by again making our perspectives fully centripetal, converging on the eternal light which is God.

To "taste of the heavenly gifts and become partakers of the Holy Spirit" (Heb 6: 4) is the goal of Christian living. To achieve it, we must become vessels of divine grace, engender "the blazing fire" (Ps 103: 4) in our souls, be "fixed on things divine," as the Secret prayer of the Mass against the persecutors of the Church puts it. If the spring of living water is kept alive, there never will be a drought. If on the other hand the spring has become a mere spurt, the effectiveness of our efforts to fertilize the pastures of our soul is bound to become questionable.

St. Macarius, the *Golden Legend* tells us, once found a skull in the desert sand.

"Whose head have you been?" he asked.

"A pagan's," the voice came back from the skull.

"And where is thy soul?"

"In Hell!"

"How deep in Hell?"

"As deeply down as the earth is lower than Heaven."

"Are there," the Saint finally asked, "any souls thrust down into Hell even more deeply than yours?"

"Yes," the voice of the skull replied. "The souls of those who were redeemed by Jesus Christ, but held their privilege cheaply."

Christians who do not want to be classed among those holding their privilege cheaply cannot help but concentrate on that inner voice to which perhaps they have not been listening with sufficient attention. Is it not a consoling thought that they can become true reformers by being non-conformers? The redemption of mankind always depends on the few who in the midst of the world's turmoil know how to practice silence with God.

Such silence entails a *metanoia*, a change of heart, a turning away from things ephemeral to things eternal, and the turn must be resolute. We cannot, as Irenaeus once expressed it, be *"mate hexo mate eso,"* which means: neither within nor without. We must be within first, then only can we be without as well. Only if we do not remain merely human beings, but keep alive in ourselves the conviction that we are truly images of God, can we achieve spiritual maturity. What else could spiritual maturity be but holiness? What could holiness really mean if not being whole, fully developed by attaining the realm of the spirit?

There is that wonderful phrase in the letter to the Ephesians (1: 23) which sums up all this in the statement that the Church is the body of Christ, "the fullness of him who is wholly fulfilled in all." St. Paul has expressed the same thought when he said that we "should bear the likeness of the heavenly as we have born the likeness of the earthy" (1 Cor 15: 49). That and no other is the program of the inner life. It means the integration of our lives in the life of God, becoming "one spirit with him" (1 Cor 6: 17).

Archabbot Baur shows in this book how such teachings can be applied in practice. From a lifetime of monastic and ascetic experience he tells us how we can "do it ourselves." And he bids us to have courage, just as our Lord said to His disciples: "Be not afraid, little flock" (Luke 12: 32). If we will but "lower our net" (Luke 5: 4) at His word, "a catch" will be ours, namely, a deeper insight into our faith. Then we will tap its sources, reach its innermost precincts.

Clearly this purpose cannot be achieved if we attempt to ride two horses, to carry water on both shoulders, to be on good terms with God and the godless world at the same time. We must be determined to choose with Mary of Bethany "the best part" always, "the only thing that is needful" (Luke 10: 42). Neutralism in this confused age will never do. We must be "stewards of the mysteries of God" (1 Cor 4: 1) and face the challenge which is ours today. By grasping its full significance we should become wholehearted followers rather than being just perfunctory, half-hearted believers.

Only in practicing that "silence with God" which Archabbot Benedict Baur so eloquently and with such deep conviction propounds, dare we hope to become partners of God in "renewing the face of the earth" (Ps 103: 30).

Placid Jordan, O.S.B.
Beuron, Germany
Feast of the Epiphany, 1960

1. *The Call*

I am come, that they may have life.
JOHN 10: 10

WHAT ARE we expected to do? What is the true purpose of our existence, our life as human beings and as Christians?

That is the crucial question, but only a revelation from God Himself can answer it infallibly. He answers it for us on every page of Holy Writ—the Old as well as the New Testament. It comes back always to the one great truth: our calling and our destiny to share in the rich beatitude of life in God the Father, the Son, and the Holy Spirit.

I. WE ARE CALLED BY GOD TO PARTICIPATE IN HIS DIVINE LIFE

The ultimate purpose of our life towers immeasurably above the natural human sphere of consciousness and experience, beyond the power of our limited human intellect to grasp or imagine. By the grace of God we are appointed—thanks to His promised gifts of redemption, purification, forgiveness—to escape "the corruption that is in the world through lust" (2 Pet 1: 3–4); to become "participators in the divine nature" and simultaneously in divine life, which, anticipating its complete unfolding in Heaven, we may even here on earth savor in reality and in truth. The secret lies in the mysterious union with God that is the whole foundation of Christianity.

"I am come," He who was made man assures us, "that they [humanity] may have life, and may have it more abundantly" (Jn 10: 10). It is not the life of this world, which we receive from our earthly parents—that life which we protect with all our strength against the power of death, only to be inevitably conquered by death in the end. The life that Christ wishes to give us is the life of God. It is the life the Son of God—as God made man—took with Him into His earthly form and flows from Him perpetually in the mystery of His Church, reaching those who are His through the sacraments. "And of his fullness have all we received" (Jn 1: 16).

God is the Living One. His superabundance of life forces Him to share all His inherent gifts, His riches, even life itself, with man, the nonentity, the dust. For this is the very nature of all that is great, good, and noble: it has the urge to pour itself into other beings, to make them rich, exalted, happy. God desired to realize a sublime idea in me as He measured out my allotted span of life and traced its definite direction. Everything in my existence points to my being lifted to the level of divine life so that I may share it and live it with my Maker.

When we speak of sharing God's life, we do not mean that we are on an equality with the Creator or that we cease to be His creatures—nor that a part of the Divine Being or a portion of His life pours itself into the individual and becomes his own property. Nor do we suggest that we carry the life of God within us in the same sense or degree as the eternal Son of God, created out of the substance of the Father and "perfect as his Father is perfect." What we mean is that with the power of His love (His sanctifying grace) God drops into our soul a quality through which we partake of the beauty, purity, and holiness that are attributes only of the divine nature. A soul that has taken on so much of the likeness of God can be fittingly described in the terms used by the Fathers of the Church: godly and god-formed. Such a soul is the reflection of the beauty, the holiness, and the fullness that set God apart from all creation, raising Him infinitely above all else and belonging to Him alone.

When the divine life pours itself into our soul, we undergo an experience, so the Fathers of the Church tell us, similar to that of iron thrust into the fire; it remains iron but loses its natural hardness and color, receiving in return the shimmer, the glow, and the heat of fire—phenomena that pertain to fire and not to iron at all. So the soul, thanks to sanctifying grace, receives a new and exalted quality, lifting it far above its natural state: a quality that transforms it to the likeness of God and enables it to share divine life even if only in a finite, created form of fulfillment. Though this new and higher quality is something created and quite different from the life of God, it raises the soul immensely above our human nature and even above the nature of angels, putting us in an entirely new relation to God, to ourselves, to our fellow men, to the world in general, and to life itself.

In this sense, and this sense alone, we may interpret the words "divine life in us," so much used—and misused—nowadays.

Divine life is within our reach; indeed we are commanded to participate in it, even though, by virtue of original sin, we are "children of wrath" (Eph 2: 3), "vessels of wrath fitted for destruction" (Rom 9: 12). By His unfailing grace God has transformed us into "vessels of mercy, which he hath prepared unto glory" (Rom 9: 23). We participate in divine life:

(a) In the everlasting glory of Heaven.

There we will find fulfillment of the promise: "Behold the tabernacle of God is with men and he will dwell with them . . . and be their God. And God shall wipe away all tears from their eyes; and death shall be no more, nor mourning nor crying, nor sorrow shall be any more" (Rev 21: 3–4). For God in His unending goodness has appointed that mankind shall share divine gifts exceeding all human comprehension (Vatican Council I, 3rd sess., ch. 2).

God has so created human nature that our spirit and our heart are forever reaching out to the infinite, into eternity.

Only in God can we find peace. Our mind strives for boundless knowledge; our heart seeks incessantly for a beloved who will endlessly and completely fulfill its longing. Our short little joys on earth forever aspire to merge in unbounded happiness.

Life eternal, which awaits us in Heaven, offers complete certainty. "That which is in part shall be put away" (1 Cor 13: 10). We shall "have life and have it more abundantly" (Jn 10: 10). We shall "be like him" (1 Jn 3: 2). Hence we shall have life like unto God, no longer as here on earth, always with only a small part of our consciousness, moment by moment, but complete in undivided wholeness and strength, corresponding with God's life, omnipresent, omnipotent, from eternity to eternity. Our spirit shall be transformed, illuminated, penetrated by a new light, a light that is kindled by the original light of the Godhead. Once lighted, its radiance and power illuminate us for evermore.

In this light we shall comprehend infinity—we will see Him "as he is" (1 Jn 3: 2), unveiled and clear in everlasting glory—not in a continual groping search as here on earth, step by step, but in eternal and complete fulfillment. Then, too, the patchwork of love will be at an end. We shall enter into the glow of divine love, attracted and absorbed by it. We shall live in an eternal, unified, uninterrupted act of love, like that of God; in the glow of divine love, our love will be made new. In godly fashion we will love with unlimited strength everything that He embraces in Himself, everything that He loves and has lovingly created.

Who can grasp all that God will make of mankind despite our dust-sprung unworthiness! We can only marvel and give thanks. This is how it will be in the future life, in the joy of Heaven, for which we are ordained.

(b) In the life here on earth.

But even here on earth we are privileged to share God's life. "For as the Father hath life in himself; so hath he given to the

Son also to have life in himself" (Jn 5: 26)—one and the same life with the Father. The divine life lives in the Son in its original, uninterrupted, unlimited, eternal fullness. "And the Word was made flesh and dwelt among us . . . full of grace and truth . . . and of his fullness have all we received, and grace for grace" (Jn 1: 14–16).

The stream of God's life pours into the Word, the Son. "God of God, light of light, true God of true God." He becomes man, and the stream of God-life flows into the created world—first through the Son of God, born of the blessed Virgin Mary, "full of grace and truth." The Son of God, by merging His divinity in the nature of man, becomes the vine, as He describes Himself. "I am the vine; you the branches; he that abideth in me, and I in him, the same beareth much fruit" (Jn 15: 5). The vine carries in itself the life that flows into the branches. Thus we, the branches, carry in ourselves the Christ-life through our union with Christ, the vine. What is human in our nature is not extinguished but immeasurably enhanced by this merging in the life of Christ. "He that abideth in me, and I in him, the same beareth much fruit."

God's Son was made man and crucified in order that we might share the gift of God's life. By His passion He severed the bonds that kept us enchained to sin and death; His sacrifice made us coheirs in divine life. So great was the love of the Father that He did not spare His only-begotten Son to achieve this end: "that whosoever believeth in him should not perish but have eternal life."

This divine life Christ the God-man earned for us through His death on the cross. "In the death of Christ, death itself perished; for he, the Life, by his death conquered Death. The fullness of Life swallowed up Death" (St. Augustine, *In Joh., Tract* 12). Life, the fruit of the crucifixion, becomes ours through our link with Christ, and this link is forged by faith, by the sacrament of Baptism. "Amen, Amen, I say to thee," our Lord declared to Nicodemus, "unless a man be born again of water and the Holy Spirit he cannot enter into the kingdom of God" (Jn 3: 5). The sacrament of Baptism is the rebirth (1 Pet 1: 23): "not of blood, nor of the will of the flesh, nor of the will of man, but of God" (Jn 1: 13; 3: 9; 4: 7; 5: 4). Through water and the Holy Spirit we are reborn coheirs of divine life. We are "new creatures," "the new man" (Eph 4: 24), sharing the divine life that is ours as "children of God."

The foundations laid in Baptism are steadily developed and amplified in the sacrament of Holy Eucharist. Holy Communion brings to us the Lord in person, as God and man. "I am come that they may have life, and may have it more abundantly." God's wish is to give us daily more and more of His life; to let us enter this very day more deeply than ever into His will for us, His thought, His awareness, His love; to pray and to offer ourselves with Him, so that, in this complete sharing of His life, we can truly say: "I live, but no longer I—rather, Christ lives in me." Holy Eucharist is the bread that "cometh down from Heaven and giveth life to the world" (Jn 6: 33). "He that eateth my flesh and drinketh my blood hath everlasting life; and I will raise him up in the last day" (Jn 6: 54).

We are deeply moved as we contemplate the mystery of our vocation to share the gift of divine life. How incomparably greater is the boon of divine life than any desire we can formulate in our human existence, whether on the physical or the mental plane! What are talent, genius, knowledge, possessions, success, health, physical strength, temporal power, high positions among our fellow men, or any other human achievement compared to this inestimable blessing? Yet we seldom sufficiently appreciate this gift of God enough to rate it at its true value, and indeed many of us will throw away the only thing worth having, our share in the life of God, in order to pursue some worthless, evanescent earthly desire. "Lord, forgive them, they know not what they do!"

2. WE ARE CALLED BY GOD TO LIVE HIS LIFE
WITH HIM

We truly possess God's divine life, even if only in a limited degree. But this sharing of God's life involves responsibilities. The mere fact of possession obliges us to live that life, to insure its unfolding and development. In fact, we can be copartners with God in His life only by living it in accordance with His intention of fulfillment. The benefit we derive from sharing God's life is that our spirit merges with God's. One spirit can only absorb another through the fulfillment of its life principles. Recognizing this, we perceive an added splendor in our call. Copartnership in God's life involves nothing less than divine awareness and knowledge—the conscious surrender to God's will and love in order to live His life with Him.

To live God's life, to think God's thoughts, to do His will and accomplish His works—what a wonderful destiny! This means, however, that our life shall no longer move on the natural human plane of thought, judgment, will, and deed; it automatically becomes a "supernatural" life, a life lifted immeasurably above the level of ordinary human experience. It is tuned in to the infinitely rich, powerful, holy life of God, Who lives in the sanctified soul and irradiates it with His light, His purity, His abhorrence of all that is unholy and wicked, with His thoughts, His strength, His love, and His joy. Whereupon the soul, not only in its substance but in all its activities, its emotions and institutions, its wish and will, its sensations and judgments, its every attitude, becomes Godlike, a true image of God, a revelation and a reflection of the life of God.

That is the mystery of the saints. They succeeded in discovering a way of living in His grace, of merging their whole being in the God-life they glimpsed in the Holy of Holies of their own souls, not merely as a thing to imitate but to link up with as the branches are linked with the vine, organically united to the parent stem and reproducing its attributes in every expression. This is our sublime purpose in life—to live the radiant, holy, glorious life of God with Him.

To live God's life with Him . . . for this alone Almighty God, the Father, the Son, and the Holy Spirit, condescends to the level of our human soul, sets up His tent there, and takes up His abode. God in residence . . . God the Father, the Son, and the Holy Spirit leading in the sanctified soul the same glorious life as in Heaven. God gives Himself to the soul, filling it with the fullness of His light, strength, holiness, and drawing it with all its yearnings into the ineffable glory of His own life.

The soul has no choice but to surrender itself to the God-life in its depths, at one with the eternal rhythm of the divine creative force. Thus it becomes more and more transformed into the likeness of the Creator and rises higher and higher above natural human life with its weaknesses, its limitations, its leaning to the low, earthly, transient. It cuts itself adrift from the disorderly ties binding it to human personality and environment and day by day takes on a more perfect approach to the Godlike way of life. In the words of St. Paul: "In all things let us exhibit ourselves as the ministers of God, in much patience, in tribulation, in necessities, in distresses, in stripes, in prisons, in seditions, in labors, in watchings, in fastings, in chastity, in knowledge, in long-suffering, in sweetness, in the Holy Spirit, in charity unfeigned, in the word of truth, in the power of God, by the armor of justice on the right hand and on the left; . . . as sorrowful, yet always rejoicing; as needy, yet enriching many; as having nothing, and possessing all things" (2 Cor 6: 4–10). Happy are those who have learned to live the life of God this way—the true Christian life.

The clearest example of the way in which this God-life should be lived is demonstrated for us by the Son of God made man, Jesus Christ. His thought and will, His acts and sufferings, His prayers and sacrifices—in short, all His teachings—constitute the pattern of God living in man, and of man's own world. Hence God's command to us: "This is my beloved Son in whom I am well pleased: hear ye Him!" (Mt 17: 5). Hence His gathering us around Him with the words "learn of me." Whoever elects to lead the life of God with Him chooses poverty, dependence upon the will of others, obscurity and humility, self-denial, the cross, self-effacement, a life of silence and of prayer—precisely those things which natural man tries with might and main to escape from. "Learn of me. . . ."

This is our calling: conformed "to the image of His Son" (Rom 8: 29). "Put ye on the Lord Jesus Christ" (Rom 13: 14). "And as we have borne the image of the earthly [Adam], let us bear also the image of the heavenly [Christ]" (1 Cor 15: 49). The more we develop in ourselves the likeness to Christ and follow His teaching, the more we will approach Godlikeness. Following Christ in our daily life is the very cornerstone of Christianity, to the end that we may live as God lives and become "perfect" as our Father is perfect.

In order that we may truly fashion our daily activities to the divine pattern and reap the full reward, Christ the Lord takes us up into His own life and makes us limbs of His own body, branches of Himself, the vine. "I am the vine; you the branches. As the branch cannot bear fruit of itself unless it abides in the vine, so neither can you unless you abide in me. He that abideth in me, and I in him, the same beareth much fruit; for without me, you can do nothing" (Jn 15: 4–5). He has incorporated us with Him in holy Baptism so that we may share His life, and with every Holy Communion He fortifies this union, giving us the aid we need to overcome our human limitations and to acquire more and more of His life—the vitality of the vine whose life the branch shares and carries on.

By His grace God has endowed our souls in Baptism with an abundance of supernatural gifts, including the three theological virtues of faith, hope, and love, as well as the

principles of wisdom, justice, courage, temperance, and a
number of others that accompany sanctifying grace—such
as veneration, humility, chastity, patience, and obedience.
These supernatural virtues, mere seeds at first, take root in
our soul and gather strength, thanks to which we are aided
in warding off evil and enabled to meet with a kind of Godlike confidence the trials of everyday existence—that is to
say, in a manner far superior to the frame of mind in which
the merely natural man views, judges, and conducts his daily
life: a manner based on that which God Himself brings to
bear in judging and evaluating man's thoughts, intentions,
and deeds.

Fundamental to all this is the virtue of faith. By faith we
rise immeasurably superior to the power and the light of human reason, for it illumines reason in a supernatural way and
gives it the power to associate itself with God's perception
and judgment—to see with God's own eyes. Faith joins our
spirit so closely to God's spirit that our perception and judgment take on a certain similarity to the wisdom, judgment,
and perception of God. Thus the act of faith surmounts all
natural human knowledge and capacity; it is a supernatural
act of participation in the wisdom of God, a "seeing with
God's eyes," a means of measuring conclusions and values by
God's standard.

It is faith, and faith alone, that substantiates the beatitudes
of the Sermon on the Mount, theoretically—and practically,
too, when they have been proved—the beatitude of the poor
in spirit, the long-suffering, those that mourn, the peace-
makers, the reviled, the outlawed, the persecuted. An attitude that by purely natural processes of arriving at an opinion
cannot be reconciled at all.

Then, there is the virtue of hope. If we strive to accomplish something seemingly too great for our human capacity—to avoid some evil or to lead a truly Christian life—we
fully realize that our human powers are inadequate for the
task. "Not that we are sufficient to think anything of our-

selves as of ourselves; but our sufficiency is from God" (2 Cor 3: 5). Yet we recognize with the Apostle: "I can do all things through Christ which strengtheneth me." That is the Christian's secret; the less he relies upon his own human power, the more the might of God is at his disposal. The more he reckons with the help and power, the loyalty and grace of God, humbly recognizing and acknowledging his own unimportance, the more he discovers that God Himself is at work, and he can say with the same Apostle: "Power is made perfect in infirmity. Gladly therefore will I glory in my infirmities, in reproaches, in necessities, in persecutions, in distress, for Christ. For when I am weak, then am I powerful" (2 Cor 12: 9–10). In this Christ-weakness God's almighty power reveals itself. The Christian who applies supernatural thought and attaches himself in complete dependence to the power of Christ in God may confidently appropriate the words of the Apostle: "I can do everything."

"And now there remain faith, hope, and charity, these three; but the greatest of these is charity [love]" (1 Cor 13: 13). In Baptism love becomes a new, divine quality—a part of God's own love. It takes on the radiance and purity of the divine nature and incorporates the attributes that belong to the Creator alone.

God loves Himself and all His creation; Himself as the good that embraces the sum of all the good there is, to infinity; His creation likewise, first for His own sake, and secondly as the reflection of His own nature, in which He recognizes Himself again and finds all good.

Christianity raises us to this quality of love; we love God for His own sake—and we love creation, in all its forms, likewise for God's sake. Hence Christian love is drawn into the infinitely holy love with which God loves and takes on the same quality. It is a truly "supernatural" love, immeasurably superior to the merely natural variety, estimable though this may be, and certainly not to be compared to the unclean, sensual urge that so often passes by the name of love. Of

Christian love (that is to say, the love with which God loves), it is written that it is "poured forth in our hearts by the Holy Spirit, who is given to us" (Rom 5: 5).

Can we wonder, then, that Christian love is so strong, so mighty, so pure, so heroic, so all-conquering? Love "is patient, is kind; love envieth not, love dealeth not perversely, is not puffed up; is not ambitious, seeketh not her own, is not provoked to anger, thinketh no evil; rejoiceth not in iniquity but rejoiceth with the truth; beareth all things, believeth all things, hopeth all things, endureth all things" (1 Cor 13: 4–7). Christian love owes this exalted quality to the fact of its being part of God's love. It so penetrates and captivates our human will that we become willing to dissolve all our desire in the will of God—to merge our yearning in the pure and infinitely reassuring acceptance of God's will for us. Surely there can be no greater happiness than this wholehearted surrender.

Yet the Christian call means even more than this. Baptism bestows upon us sanctifying grace and supernatural virtues—the gifts of the Holy Spirit: wisdom and understanding, good counsel, piety, knowledge, strength, and fear of the Lord. Due to original sin, the imperfection of our human nature hinders it from reaching out to supernatural perfection. The inner urge is lacking to reach the highest goal. So God has planted the gifts of the Holy Spirit in our soul to provide the motive force that, combating our natural incapacity, perpetually impels us to scale the pinnacle of Christian fulfillment.

We are actuated by an entirely new driving force: no longer hemmed in by human limitations but carried away by the power of the Holy Spirit—like a boat that need no longer rely upon its oars, since its sails, swelling in the wind, propel it effortlessly. Similarly impelled by the Holy Spirit, we are able to overcome and to accomplish in a manner that passes all human reason, and we realize, as never before, how truly our own limited power has been merged in the almighty power of God. It is precisely in arriving at the pinnacle of his calling, in performing his holiest and most heroic works, that the Christian realizes they are not his works at all, but God's. "He that glorieth, may glory in the Lord" (1 Cor 1: 31); "Who worketh in you both to will and to accomplish, according to His goodwill" (Phil 2: 13).

The culminating issue of the call, to perceive, to accept the divine will and to do the divine works—in short, to share God's life and live it—follows hereafter in Heaven. "For now we see through a glass in a dark manner, but then face to face. Now I know in part, but then I shall know even as I am known" (1 Cor 13: 12). To know God even as He is, in the wholeness of His Being, His perfection, His wisdom, His justice and mercy, His purity and holiness, His unending fruitfulness expressed in three divine Persons. This perception of God is the ultimate rapture of love, a love such as we can never know here on earth—full of wonder, gratitude, innocence, and deep intimacy, a love in which above all we rejoice that God, the holiest of holies, exists; a love in which we wonderingly adore the eternal decrees of His providence, crying in exultation "Holy, Holy, Holy."

But how is this vision of God and the eternal ecstasy of love possible? Only by the fact that God permits us to partake of His nature, so that we may participate in His manner of knowing, loving, and living. We are born of God, "partakers of the divine nature" (2 Pet 1: 4) and truly "sons of God" and "joint-heirs with Christ" (Rom 8: 16-17).

Thus we raise ourselves to the final heights. The end is not man but God—that His name may be hallowed, His will be done. All that man is—all that he possesses in gifts of nature and grace, of virtue and holiness, his life, his fate, his property—is but a means to the ultimate and highest; the glorification of God. The more we share God's life, the more we will exalt Him in our works and sufferings, our thoughts and intentions. Our incessant aim will be to love Him, to acknowledge His abundant gifts, and, filled with

His inexpressible bliss, to praise and serve Him lovingly for all eternity.

Truly God's intentions for poor, benighted mankind are unutterably good. This is the purpose of His commandments. The trials and tribulations He allows man in this life on earth are but means to draw us to His final reward, because only by this challenge can we be induced to make the necessary effort to attain the goal He has prepared for us.

And what of us? We spare so little time to think over the meaning of all this. We have so little appreciation of the Almighty's intentions. We forget all that we owe to the Son of God. Had He not taken His cross upon Him, wiping away with His death the sins of the world, we should be forever condemned to death and darkness. "I am come that ye may have life, and may have it more abundantly" (Jn 10: 10).

2. For God

So do you also reckon that you are dead to sin, but alive unto God.
ROMANS 6: 11

To LIVE God's life with Him—that is our exalted calling. God, however, lives His own life. He has an end and a purpose in Himself—not like us, who must look for fulfillment outside ourselves. All the good there is, every good that can be desired to infinity, is incorporated in Him. This wholeness is so complete that it cannot be increased or enhanced by any good beyond itself. If other things exist outside of God, they are only revelations, reflections of Himself—emanations of the abundance of omnipresent good, each individual one of them a mere nothing in comparison with Him. Thus the Almighty in the infinity of His goodness is the sum total of all good, sufficient unto Himself and ceaselessly expressing Himself in His omnipresent, all-good life. We coexist with Him, therefore we also live for Him, entirely for Him.

I. THE FACT: WE LIVE FOR GOD

(a) We coexist in God's life with Jesus Christ, the vine whose branches we have become. "For in that he died to sin, he died once; but in that he liveth, he liveth unto God" (Rom 6: 10). His life on earth was life for God. "I seek not my own glory" (Jn 8: 50). "My meat is to do the will of him that sent me" (Jn 4: 34). "He that sent me . . . I do always the things that please him" (Jn 8: 29). When the Apostle sets out to describe the Son of God made man, he can find no more fitting expression than the Word. He became "obedient unto death, even to the death of the cross" (Phil 2: 3). He lived the life of the Father as long as he remained here on earth. He still lives the will, the honor, the desires, and intentions of the Father day by day in the tabernacles of our churches. His life is a complete surrender to the Father. In the daily sacrifice of the altar He raises us, the limbs of His Mystical Body, into the rarer essence of His devotion and praise of the Father. So perfect is His identity with the life of the Father that He has but one desire—to intensify and increase the life of God in us.

(b) It is for this reason that he has taken up His abode in us in Baptism. From our parents we receive human love; but they cannot prevent our being drawn into original sin the moment they give us life. If the Lord did not lift us up into His life we should remain "in the desires of our flesh, fulfilling the will of the flesh . . . But God, who is rich in mercy . . . even when we were dead in sins hath [in his great love, in Baptism] quickened us together in Christ" (Eph 2: 3–5). In Baptism we renounce sin and the world with its lusts and vanities. Everything that separates us from God we forswear. We are asked: "Do you believe in the Father, the Son, and the Holy Spirit?" And we answer: "I believe." We acknowledge God, take His side. With our whole being, awareness, and will, we yield ourselves to God the Father, the Son, and the Holy Spirit. Then in the name of God the Father, the Son, and the Holy Spirit we are baptized. From that moment we no longer belong to ourselves, nor to any other object whatever it may be—neither to man nor beast, to treasure or talent, art, work, heritage, gold, health, beauty. We belong to God; in Christ Jesus, with Christ Jesus, we live in the Father. That is the meaning of Baptism.

(c) Baptism qualifies us to take part in the celebration of Mass. This is the kernel and the summit of Christian life. As the priest offers up the bread and wine, we place with this sacrifice upon the altar our ego—our wishes and our inclinations, everything that we have or are capable of, everything that we can do or suffer. "In the depths of humility and contrition may we find acceptance with thee, O Lord." We yearn to offer ourselves to God, united in spirit and desire with the very Lord Who is offering Himself up in the sacrament. In this sanctified moment we break with all that is not God, all that is not for Him. We renounce all self-love, all ungoverned affection for the things of the world; in this act of renunciation we are prepared for the climax of the sacrifice, with which we associate ourselves. Transubstantiation lifts us with Christ in the "holy, pure, spotless sacrifice" to God, dedicated to Him and dissolved in Him.

The new day we have started with the celebration of Mass is "holy unto God." It belongs wholly to Him. All our labors and efforts—every moment of the whole day—are His, for we have been consecrated with Christ in the Transubstantiation and live today, as He lives, in the Father. The Lord Jesus Christ Himself enters our soul in Holy Communion. "I live and you shall also" (Jn 14: 19). He floods our soul with His holy, God-begotten life. "As I live by the Father, so he that eateth me, the same also shall live by me" (Jn 6: 57). Jesus draws the soul into that love with which He loves the Father. He permits it to enter His heart, transforms it with His own radiance so that it may love the Father and live in the Father with Him and through Him. He teaches the soul and obliges it to adore Him, to praise Him, to surrender itself to Him as He Himself does. We live dependent on the life of Jesus and approach Christlikeness, making true the words, "As far as his life is concerned, he lives for God," in the spirit and the power of Jesus.

(d) Those of us who have taken religious vows must consider further implications. We have vowed ourselves to the virtue of poverty. Why?—To complete chastity. Why?—To the virtue of obedience. Why? Why have we voluntarily severed all ties to material possessions, to earthly love, to self-determination?—Only to lose ourselves completely in God's love so that we may live His life in Him.

God Himself lives in His omnipresence; we live in all with

Him. "So do you also reckon that you are dead to sin but alive unto God in Jesus Christ our Lord" (Rom 6: 11).

2. WHAT IS MEANT BY "LIVING FOR GOD"?

(a) "In that he died to sin, he died once." We enter into His life. "So do you also reckon that you are dead to sin but alive unto God in Jesus Christ our Lord." This is the first and most decisive step toward living for God—being dead to sin. Breaking not only with mortal sin but also with venial sins, all conscious untruth, trespass, and fault. Sin is always and in all its forms an offense to God. If we wish to live for God we must have no part in sin at all. We must make any sacrifice rather than lay ourselves open to conscious trespass. This means applying unshakable willpower to withdrawing from all situations that might lead to temptation. We must leave "the broad way that leadeth to destruction" (Mt 7: 13). We must never again allow ourselves to be influenced by the worldly outlook. We know that "all that is in the world, . . . the concupiscence of the eyes and the pride of life, is not of the Father but is of the world" (1 Jn 2: 16) and against God.

(b) To live for God means also to live for His creatures— for the healing of souls, the souls of others, for the family, for one's profession, for earthly progress and betterment, for duty, for learning, for bodily health, and for all that concerns the community, the State. But in all our concern about worldly duties we must never forget that our primary preoccupation should be with eternal life beyond the grave. Our vision should pass beyond material things in our immediate environment to God, on Whom our eyes must forever rest. We derive satisfaction not from ourselves but from God; not from the fulfillment of our worldly desires, from success or the honor we attain among men, not from our gains, our advantages, our progress. God in all! Living for God means nothing less than cutting ourselves adrift with heart, soul,

and mind from all the ungoverned passions that draw us to
material good, freeing the inner recesses of our being from
pride, self-love, and the attractions and repulsions that lurk
there. In this way we will attain a balanced attitude to man
and to labor, to suffering and resignation, subjecting all
things to our inner life with a proper sense of proportion.

(c) To live for God involves three things: we must see Him
in everything; we must make ourselves dependent upon
Him; and we must lovingly submit everything to Him.

To see God in everything, glorifying Him. "Hallowed be thy
name." "The Lord hath made all things for himself" (Prov
16: 4), for the glorification of His name. Just as it is impossible for anything to exist without His having created it, so it
is equally impossible for anything to exist for a purpose other
than that of glorifying God, reflecting His image, bearing
witness to His greatness. The honor and the glory of God is
the purpose of all creation. And it is also the purpose we
must have in mind if we wish really to live for God and not
for ourselves.

But in order to perceive God, it is necessary to see Him in
everything. What we need above all things is the eye of faith,
which sees in everything the day brings not only the workings of nature, of good and bad influences, or of evilly dis-
posed persons but the hand, the providence, the ordinance
of God. It is He who orders and guides, He who gives and
takes away, He the great reality we recognize in every event
and circumstance.

To make oneself dependent upon God in everything. Living for
God, we are no longer affected by anything else; only the will
of God is operative in our lives. God's commandments and
will are our norm and guiding principle. No longer do we
desire anything that would offend God, anything that would
be inconsistent with His will and commandments. Gladly do
we relinquish all our own desires and affections to lose ourselves entirely in what is pleasing to him. With faith and
confidence we submit to the sanctions, ordinances, and de-

crees of Providence, yielding up all resistance in the inner and outer life, and saying in loving humility: "Not as I will, but as thou wilt. Thy will be done."

To love God in everything. Fear of God is the beginning of wisdom, life's unfolding. But fulfillment rests in love. Love alone makes it possible to forget everything else and offer ourselves entirely to God. Love makes God all-in-all to us, the sun around which we revolve. Love directs our thoughts and intentions to God. It enables us to see Him in everything, to meet Him in everything, to hear His voice in everything, to live with Him in all things and relate everything to His will. Love enables us to dedicate all our wishes and desires to Him, turning from all other allegiance and even subordinating our natural human affections and our work in His service. It forces us to look first to God in all things, raising us above self-love and human frailty. It makes us strong to accept the trials and tribulations of daily life with quiet resignation, indeed, with grateful joy. To everything that gives and takes, love has only one answer: "For Thee, O Lord, out of love for Thee." God, His holy will, His pleasure. . . .

For love, nothing else is of any account. That is why love subordinates ruthlessly all other considerations, everything we think, desire, do, or leave undone. Love must rule supreme. It is the flame that rises to Heaven, illuminating everything in us that it can reach—our prayers, our work, our renunciations, our sufferings, our sacrifices. We no longer live for ourselves, for any other person, for our achievements, our duty, our profession. We live altogether in God, for the will and the pleasure of God. God alone! That is the function of love.

"Reckon ye also yourselves to be dead unto sin, but alive unto God."

It is our appointed task, every moment of the day, to live for God. "I am the Lord thy God . . . thou shalt not have strange gods before me" (Ex 20: 2–3). No other gods! In religion there are no half-measures. A man either recognizes

God as All, or he looks upon himself as the sun around which the universe revolves; so much so that he regards all others, and even God Himself, as being there for *his* convenience. God or ego! Whoever refuses to live for God makes this choice.

"To live for God in Christ Jesus! . . ." God, the almighty and eternal, gives Himself to us in the wholeness of His being and calls us to His immediate service. Compared to this, every other service is petty, unworthy, of no account. What an honor for man!

To live for God. . . . Herein lies our true greatness and our genuine worth, for these are not measured by outward works and achievements, by titles, honors, position, nor by the glory accruing from talent, learning, success. It can be judged only by the goal that life attains. He who strives for the higher goal is the greater. He who lives for God and serves Him in all things is the greatest.

To live for God. . . . Therein lies mankind's only true happiness. In His wonderful wisdom and goodness God has bound up my life in His. I can be happy only insofar as I live for Him, surrendering myself to His will, to His honor, obeying His decrees and serving Him to His good pleasure. "Thou hast created us, and our heart is disquieted (and unhappy) until it rests in Thee." St. Augustine proved the truth of these, his own words, as few others have done.

To live for God. . . . Whatsoever in me is not directed to living for Him, serving Him to His honor and glory—my love of self or of another human being, my work, my regard for honor among men, my preoccupation with business or gain, with health and comfort—are vanity, madness, and loss. Only what is done, offered, or accomplished for the will of God and His glory has any sense or value.

$$\star \quad \star \quad \star$$

FOR WHOM do I live? Whom do I serve? To whom do my thoughts, my secret wishes and inclinations, my exertions and efforts belong? Truly to God? Not to myself? Not for my own honor? Do I live for God in everything, even in striving after virtue, holiness, piety? And in the service of souls, the upbringing of the young, the instruction of adults? Really for God? In nothing for myself? Everything entirely for Him, for His honor, for His will? That is the important question.

3. *Be You Perfect*

Be you therefore perfect, as also your heavenly Father is perfect.
MATTHEW 5: 48

WE ARE to share God's life with Him. This brings us face to face with the almost frightening command "Be you therefore perfect, as also your heavenly Father is perfect" (Mt 5: 48). "Ye have heard that it was said to them of old: Thou shalt not kill; and whosoever shall kill shall be in danger of the judgment. . . . Thou shalt not commit adultery. . . . Thou shalt not forswear thyself. . . . Thou shalt love thy neighbor and hate thy enemy. But I say to you, that whosoever is angry with his brother shall be in danger of the judgment; that whosoever shall look on a woman to lust after her hath already committed adultery with her in his heart. . . . Swear not at all, but let your speech be Yea, yea, no, no . . . , love your enemies, do good to them that hate you. . . . That you may be the children of your Father who is in Heaven, who maketh his sun to rise upon the good and bad and raineth upon the just and the unjust. Be you therefore perfect, as also your heavenly Father is perfect" (Mt 5: 21–48). "I am the LORD your God. . . . You shall be holy, because I am holy" (Lev 11: 44-46).

I. THE COMMAND

By virtue of Baptism the Christian carries supernatural, "sanctifying" grace in his soul. This is the seed, the root, of supernatural life. As every healthy seed carries within itself the urge to grow and unfold, so also with the sanctifying grace within us. Every baptized person comes under the law of impulse to growth and fulfillment. Should a man try to escape this law and refuse to grow, he would necessarily wither and decline. As every created life encounters disturbing forces that seek to hinder its development, so, too, there are many evil elements threatening the existence of supernatural life. Anyone who is not earnestly concerned with fostering his supernatural life must eventually succumb to these disturbing forces.

That is why we must never hesitate but go on and on. The fundamental duty of every Christian is to press earnestly toward the goal of perfection, to become more perfect moment by moment. Only in this way can he preserve his supernatural life and ensure its unfolding.

Be perfect. . . . With inexpressible love the Lord has taken us up into His own life in the sacrament of Baptism, "that we may partake of his divine nature" (Pet 1: 4). In addition to the supernatural life principle of sanctifying grace, He has given us the three divine virtues of faith, hope, and love, as well as feet to carry us to Him, arms with which to receive Him, and a plenitude of so-called moral virtues, such as justice, prudence, strength, and temperance, with which to circumvent the daily influence of earthly things and thus strengthen the gifts of the Holy Spirit (which are actually the supernatural prerequisites for a perfect, holy life).

Grafted to Christ, the vine, in Baptism, we automatically become children of the Church—ours the holy, God-inspired writings of the Old and New Testament; ours the sacraments; ours the mystery of Christ in the blessed Eucharist as sacrifice and spiritual nourishment; ours the rewards and virtues, the prayers and satisfactions of Christ in His holy, pure, God-loving soul in Heaven and on earth. Yes, in Baptism God Himself, Father, Son, and Holy Spirit, lovingly takes residence in our soul, to be near to us, to draw us into His divine life, and secretly to copy and develop it in us. It is therefore not only possible but indeed imperative for us to become perfect as our Father in Heaven is perfect.

Just as Baptism is the sacrament of rebirth, so Confirmation is the sacrament of fulfillment. As at Pentecost, the Holy Spirit descended upon the apostles, so He descends upon us Christians in Confirmation, bringing us the strength to bear testimony for Christ. How shall we bear testimony for Christ?—Primarily by leading a life "dead unto the sins of the world," then by allowing the intentions and virtues of Christ to light up in us, that we may become like another Christ, ready to make every sacrifice and put forth every effort to resist all things that might be contrary to our union with God. In the sacrament of Confirmation we receive the power and strength to attain maturity and perfection in Christian life. Confirmation compels us to take the first faltering steps toward Christian fulfillment: "Be ye perfect."

Ever anew, we are called to assist in the sacrifice of the Mass, that we may actively participate in the offering up of Christ, uniting ourselves with Him in the offering. Whenever we receive the Holy Eucharist worthily, or assist in the sacrifice with the officiating priest, we renew the redemption Christ earned for us on the cross. With complete acquiescence we join in His sacrifice, making His intentions and His objects our own. When our Lord, in Holy Communion, gives Himself for our soul's nourishment, He fills us to the depths of our being with His spirit and His sacrificial power. Then we become strong to cope with our daily tasks, all our efforts and strivings permeated with the Christ-spirit of surrender to the glory of God.

The Christian turns his entire day into one unbroken sacrifice of prayer, thanksgiving, praise, and expiation by initiating it with Holy Communion, offering up everything that God's will has imposed upon him to do, endure, or suffer. Participation in Mass gives us daily opportunity to enter more fully into our Lord's spirit of sacrifice, into His surrender to the Father, into His obedience unto death. Every day it renews and intensifies our need to draw from Holy Communion the courage and strength to unite ourselves in an innermost spiritual wholeness with Christ, completely absorbed in His will, so that we may offer ourselves totally with Him and fulfill the command: "Be you perfect."

Be you perfect. . . . In the first place, this means fulfilling God's will to His honor and glory. Who makes the most imperative demand for the honor of God? Who surrenders himself completely, without reserve, to the guidance and providence of God? He who is perfect. One perfect soul glorifies God more than thousands of imperfect souls. For a single act of love on the part of a perfect soul is more pleasing to God than the sum total of all the incomplete acts of love proffered by those who have not reached perfection. But the perfect soul is constantly occupied in such acts of perfect love. If, therefore, we wish truly and eagerly to worship God, our constant aim must be to rise above our shortcomings and reach perfection.

Be you perfect. . . . In the second place, it means the well-being of our soul. How can we best ensure this?—By genuinely and effectively striving for perfection. The more we occupy ourselves with the attainment of perfection, the more surely we will guard ourselves against sin, against every sin, however unimportant it may seem. He who wrestles for perfection withstands the many opportunities and temptations that lead to evil. He never loses sight of the ideal spurring him on, leaving him no peace. He has no time for half-measures.

Be you perfect. . . . We need saints in these times. On every hand we hear it said that conditions in the world today are hopeless and cannot go on. What can save the world today?—Only holiness, the holiness of Christians, above all of priests and those who have taken religious vows. We need perfect Christians, perfect priests, perfect monks and nuns, perfect fathers and mothers, students, officials, workers, and employers. If anyone wishes to render a true service to the world, to the Church, to his country, to mankind, to himself, he must start with himself by subordinating everything to the pursuit and attainment of perfection.

How unchristian the life today has become . . . how worldly the spirit in the churches, in community life, in the family, in men's thoughts and hearts . . . how torn and divided is mankind today, having no deep inner relation to God and therefore drifting helpless, unhappy, bitter, bereft of true joy and courage to live. This is in spite of so much effort on the part of the ecclesiastical authorities; so many good books and writings, so many missions, congresses, sermons, speeches, yes, even confessions, Communions, pilgrimages, devout services, and religious celebrations. It is always the same bitter experience: the buildup magnificent, the results meagre and impermanent. Ever and again the Evil One arrives to sow his weeds—and the weeds choke the good seed.

In truth there is only one cure—the earnest striving for perfection, the full realization of living, active Christian virtue—in a word, Christian holiness. But this must have deep roots. Things of the outer world cannot be eliminated, but they must be centered deep within. The soul of perfection is the inner life, turning from worldliness, breaking with every conscious sin and attachment to personality, or anything other than God—anything that can hinder our union with God, our zealous practice of renunciation, contrition, atonement, our devout behavior in the presence of God, our prayer, meditation, and above all our readiness to bear, suffer, and sacrifice for the love of God. This is precisely what the present times demand of Christians, of a life of Christian perfection. Be you perfect. . . . This alone will bring us help and salvation.

2. WHEN ARE WE PERFECT?

When we love we are perfect. "Thou shalt love the Lord thy God with thy whole heart, and with thy whole soul, and with thy whole mind . . . and thy neighbor as thyself" (Mt 22: 37–39). Love is the highest expression, the ultimate term, of our capacity. In love we gather up our whole being, feeling, will, and endeavor, giving ourselves, with all that we possess and all we are capable of, to the one we love. God is glorified by love more than by anything else. Love most completely fulfills His commandments. On the commandments to love God and our neighbor "hang the whole laws and the prophets" (Mt 22: 40). All commandments and duties refer to love. Love is the fulfillment of commandments and duties; without love there is no fulfillment. It is the soul of all virtues; it is itself all virtues. If love is lacking, all is lacking. Where love is, there all things are, including all the other virtues. These virtues grow as naturally out of love as out of their own roots: they serve love and smooth its path to such an extent that the loving soul easily and readily does everything that love demands.

We are just as perfect as the love we bear. Bear to whom? —To God and to our neighbor. That is why God makes love the sign by which His disciples may be known. "By this shall all men know that you are my disciples, if you have love one for another" (Jn 13: 35), filled with My spirit, sharing My life. In the same way the Apostle measures our love for God by the love we bear to our neighbors. "For he that loveth not his brother, . . . how can he love God?" (1 Jn 4: 20). The love with which we love God and our brother in Christ is the same. Only the motive differs. We love God for His own sake; our brother, to do the will of God and Christ.

How false, how deceptive and destructive, therefore, is the conception of perfection which many people entertain. They think that perfection consists of extraordinary penances, of mortifications, of fastings, and the greatest possible sacrifices. They think they are perfect when they are free from temptation and strife, when they can pray plentifully without any trouble, when they experience comfort and sweetness in prayer, when they are able to pray just as they wish to pray. Those who have taken religious vows often think they are perfect if they follow their rules and regulations to the letter. Who would question that mortifications, zeal in prayer, and observance of rules are indispensable for spiritual perfection within the convent? They, however, are not perfection in themselves. There are many among the mortified, many ardent worshippers, many rule-abiding religious who yet are unyielding in judgment, proud and vain, obstinate and opinionated, faultfinding, lacking love in thought and speech, hypersensitive, jealous, easily put out, moody, and uncontrolled. Can these be called perfect?

We are just as perfect as the love we bear. Love is within reach of all who are in a state of sanctifying grace, who keep God's commandments, who commit no mortal sin. But is such a one truly perfect?—Not necessarily. Perfection demands more than this. It rules out not only all mortal sin but also every conscious venial sin. It declares war on every fault of which it becomes aware. It tolerates no neglect, no half-measures, no easygoing indifference, no fault of character— even though it cannot prevent man here on earth from often falling victim to unconscious weaknesses and faults of human nature.

Perfection consists particularly of doing all the good that is possible in given circumstances and situations—and not only what is commanded or cannot be omitted without committing sin. It extends beyond the sphere of duty. It does not ask: Must I do this? Is it a sin if I do it, or do not do it? Moreover, any good we have an opportunity to perform must be complete: outwardly perfect, performed in a proper and careful manner, leaving no room for the least reproach of negligence; inwardly perfect, springing from an intention of pure love, sincerely first for the sake of God's will and Christ's. But we are really perfect only when it has become a habit, second nature, to regulate our thoughts and actions entirely with reference to God, His will, His honor and glory, yielding in all things to His good pleasure.

Perfection rests upon love, that is to say, upon the complete fulfillment of the commandment: "Thou shalt love the Lord thy God with thy whole soul, with thy whole mind, and thy neighbor as thyself." Whoever loves anything more than God, whoever loves anything opposed to God, whoever loves in the same degree anything that is not God, fails to fulfill the commandment of love and consequently is not on the road to perfection. If he wishes to take the way of perfect life, he must in some measure fulfill the law of love. Christians have a wide field of endeavor in seeking perfection, since perfection, like love, has unlimited forms. Fundamentally, one may distinguish between two kinds of Christian perfection—essential perfection, and perfection in a narrower and more particular sense.

Essential perfection, which may also be described as perfection in a wider sense, is that perfection without which no one can attain the goal of Christian life—eternal life in God. This requires not only the fulfillment of the commandments (living in a state of sanctifying grace) but, over and above that, doing everything that is necessary to remain in a state of grace (thereby guarding against mortal sin). Yet if a Christian were only to do or leave undone that which he is strictly commanded by the law to do or not to do, he would still not fulfill Christ's behest, "Be you perfect." If such a one, for instance, were to bestow brotherly love only where it was indicated by strict duty, where it could not be withheld without sin, he would fulfill the law of brotherly love in only the minimum of cases. He who never goes beyond the strict letter of the law is still a long way from essential perfection.

Perfection in the particular and narrower sense—and it is this we are concerned with here—goes far beyond essential perfection. It not only fulfills the law but in addition seeks to carry out every recommendation, every good act suggested by God and Christ. Passing beyond what is strictly commanded or forbidden, this species of perfection consists of a positive eagerness to excel in the more difficult tasks, renunciations, and sacrifices. Wherever the soul may most heroically prove its love, those striving for higher perfection are to be found, performing their tasks carefully, punctually, with complete devotion, self-surrender, endurance. This is the kind of perfection at which the religious orders aim. Their whole purpose is the highest fulfillment of the commandments and the three evangelical counsels of perfection—voluntary poverty, chastity, and obedience—besides. Wrestling for perfection is so essential to the religious state that it is known as "the state of perfection," that is to say, it is a form of life in which the fulfillment of the evangelical counsels becomes a professional duty. A duty, moreover, whose highest and noblest fulfillment requires that it be done not grudgingly but in a spirit of eagerness and love, inspiring the member of a religious order to make decisions at all times from the evangelical-counsel standpoint—indeed, finding it almost impossible to do otherwise.

Whoever does not attain perfection fails in the task given to him in Baptism. After all, one who does reach the heights of Christian perfection merely makes good the vow offered up at his Baptism. There simply is no other way to be a Christian than to strive after perfection. Striving for perfection is simply the fulfillment of the baptismal vow.

Hence we are called to a life of perfection. Be you perfect. . . . Perfection consists essentially of love. The more it grows, the greater our strength to grow in love—and this in turn impels us to strive for more and more perfection. "The love of Christ holdeth us" (2 Cor 5: 14). This is the language of perfection. Perfection constrains us quickly and decisively to avoid evil and to do good to the best of our ability—even when it is not commanded, when only advice or an inner voice indicates it should be done. How could it be otherwise? After all, perfection is, essentially, nothing but love. Love, the all-consuming flame of which it has been so truly written: "Love alone makes all burdens light and endures inequality with equal courage. It endures the heaviest burdens and is not distressed by them. It makes the bitter sweet, the repulsive pleasant. It spurs to great deeds and awakens desires to accomplish even more. . . . It is fit for everything, fulfills much, and brings to pass that which those who do not love faintheartedly abandon."

*   *   *

SO WE must ask ourselves: "Are we perfect?" In prayer, in work, in obedience, in suffering, in our contacts with others? Are we perfect in relation to sin, in relation to all the good that is within our power? Are we completely loyal in zeal to strive for a greater, more pure love of God and our neighbor? In our tireless efforts for progress, growth in freedom from sin, in virtue?

4. Purification of the Heart

Blessed are the clean of heart.
MATTHEW 5: 8

To LIVE the life of God with Him means a life that is above everything created on this earth and belongs wholly to God, glorifying the will of God, the perfect love of God. That is the pinnacle to which we are called. And how to get there? We must incessantly occupy our thoughts with that question.

For thousands of years it has been customary to distinguish three different approaches to a devout life: the way of purification, the way of illumination, and the way of unity; or, in other words, the way of beginners, the way of the more advanced, and the way of the perfect. The heights of perfection are therefore two steps removed; these must be climbed before we can reach the fulfillment of love. They cannot be separated from one another or sidetracked in any way. It is not as though we could reach unity without the labor of purifying the heart, shielding it against sin and error; or as though we could dispense with illumination, the constant desire for virtue and growth in virtue. These three paths of purification, illumination, and unity are so closely linked that they converge.

Let us consider purification. "Blessed are the clean of heart. . . ."

I. THE REASON FOR PURIFICATION

To live God's life with Him in Christ Jesus. . . . He, the true vine, desires and is obliged to extend His life to us. That is the deepest meaning of our Christian life, of Christianity.

We are, as St. Paul recalls (more than a hundred and fifty times!) in his epistles, "in Christ Jesus." We are vitally joined to Him, just as the branch is joined to the vine, the hand to the arm, the arm to the body, the body to the living soul. In us Jesus wishes to reflect Himself. In us He desires to relive, as faithfully and perfectly as possible, the life He led on earth, to the glory of the Father, to the healing of our souls and the souls of others.

He, however, leads a life of the utmost purity, since He is the Son of God, God Himself. He cannot live otherwise than in a pure and holy manner. All His thoughts and wishes, His intentions and motives, are pure. His heart is pure, free from any imperfect impulse, attraction, or repulsion; free from the slightest attachment to personal judgment, personal insight, or personal will; free from all sensuality, from every sign of pride, from every form of selfishness. As divine purity, He lives in us, His limbs, and ardently desires that His purity may overcome in us all that is unclean, filling us completely. For this He gives us His example. For this He also gives us His strength. In the strength of Christ we can and must "cleanse ourselves from all defilement of the flesh and of the spirit, perfecting sanctification in the fear of God" (2 Cor 7: 1).

There is such a thing as original sin. The great corruption of the human heart from which we suffer dates back to this. Our intellect is darkened. We recognize neither God nor ourselves. Left to our own mentality we understand neither the reason for our existence nor the direction it is taking. We do not know what our true happiness consists of, neither do we know how we shall find it. We are blind and do not know we are blind; yes, we believe that we can see, although we do not see. Our will, created quite straight by our Maker, is twisted and perverse. Our heart originally had a natural urge to love God above all things. Original sin has diverted our love to ourselves. Whatever we love, we love for our own sake. We seek our own advantage, our own interest in everything. From childhood on we strive for earthly possessions and enjoyments. Hence the needs and the sensations of the body draw us so completely into their toils that they make slaves of us. Covetousness, the source of nearly all our sins, springs from original sin. It inclines us to evil. It makes it so difficult for us to desire good, still more difficult to do good. We see what is good—acknowledge, approve, and desire it— but we do evil. We are not what we ought to be. There is so much in us that should not be. What must we do about it? We must tear ourselves away daily from all disordered instinct and inclinations, from pride and sensuality, from destructive adherence to our own judgment, our own wishes, our own will, our own selfish greed.

The question of our inner progress, of our climbing the heights of a Christian life, a life with God and for God, is simply a question of purifying the heart. We get just so much grace as our heart is ready for by the cleansing it has received. The measure of benefit we can derive from Holy Communion, from prayer, from our religious life, depends entirely on our heart's state of purity—its freedom from sin, from pride, from selfishness and the love of self, from all errors of thought and desire, from the personal ego with its illusions and false values. The first step toward grace, toward progress in grace, is the purification of the heart. When our spiritual strivings come to a halt, when prayers and the sacraments no longer bear fruit, then a cleansing of the heart is indicated. This is the essential prerequisite before any progress can be made.

Hence, the work of cleansing the heart is the most fundamental task. The road of purification is the first road to take. Whoever thinks he can arrive at his destination by taking some other, more comfortable, way is making a grievous mistake. Those who wish to climb the ladder must start with the lowest rung. Without a beginning there can be no progress, no completion. First, all faults must be eliminated, all weeds rooted out, the soil prepared. The first step is the most necessary—indeed, the only one that can insure success. Of course, the labor may be frightening enough to put one off. Possibly the modern idea—"All nature is good. Let it have its way. Let the weeds grow"—sounds quite sensible. But here the words of the prophet apply: "My people, they that call thee blessed, the same deceive thee, and destroy the way of thy steps" (Is 3: 12).

In reality, only one way leads to success: the way that lies in purifying the heart. It is not sufficient in itself to achieve perfection, but it cannot be omitted. When the Virgin of Nazareth was chosen to bear the Son of God, to become the Mother of Christ, the first requirement was her purity. That is the mystery of the Immaculate Conception. When a St. Benedict, a St. Francis, a St. Gertrude, a St. Thérèse desire to mount the heights of holiness from the child Jesus, they have to wrestle constantly for complete purity of love in thoughts, intentions, and motives, following the commandment: "He that is holy, let him be sanctified still" (Rev 22: 11).

"Blessed are the clean of heart." With the Psalmist we pray: "Create a clean heart in me, O God; and renew a right spirit within me" (Ps 50: 10).

2. THE WAY TO PURIFICATION

Create a clean heart in me. . . . It is God's purpose and our duty to cleanse ourselves from all evil that we have done or that resides in us; to preserve our purity from all evil, from sin and untruth.

Naturally, this cleansing relates in the first place to every sin of sensuality, every conscious transgression, every untruth, every waste of time and grace in deliberate neglect, lack of concentration, inefficiency, in all branches of our daily life. It is therefore true that we fail and commit sin daily. Incessantly we are obliged to admit faults and ask God's pardon. Constantly we have reason to pray: "Our Father, forgive us our trespasses."

It is up to us to enter daily into the spirit of the *Confiteor*, the preparatory prayer of Mass: "I have sinned exceedingly in thought, word, and deed, through my fault, through my fault, through my most grievous fault." It is only right that we should frequently receive the sacrament of Penance. We should submit cheerfully to our daily labors and exertions, doing our duty in a spirit of contrition and atonement, taking up the burdens and the bitterness we may be called upon to bear, as though they were a cross. The spirit of penitence should permeate all our acts, spurring us on to greater fidelity, so that we may serve Him Whom we have offended with the glowing ardor of pure love.

In the second place, purification is concerned with liberating us from the bad habit of seeking first our own convenience and advantage, our own personal interests, the satisfaction of our own wishes. First ourselves, then God! Here is the gaping wound, the core of our sickness, the canker that infects the blood. We seek self first; we are selfish egoists masked in piety and deluding ourselves that we cannot know our inner motives—perhaps, if the truth were known, because we do not even want to see them. In almost every case this secret attitude renders devotion futile, being neither genuine nor sincere. We live in a kind of easygoing piety, even in our innermost heart, and find it quite easy to "pray": "Hallowed be Thy name, Thy will be done." We dedicate ourselves daily to Almighty God so that we may live entirely for Him, endure everything for His sake, devoting our life wholly to His honor and His interests. *Gloria Patri, et Filio et Spiritui Sancto.* But in everyday matters we belie our vows and our prayers. "Create in me, O Lord, a clean heart."

Another destructive habit is that of immersing ourselves in all kinds of useless, perverted, vain thoughts, making plans for the future, worrying unnecessarily. There are some things we must really worry about. God wills it so, but in moderation. And we so seldom do this in moderation! Man is so constituted that he worries about things that really do not concern him—things that come within his orbit, perhaps, but in relation to which he is powerless. He, however, does not like to feel frustrated and impotent. He looks upon himself as one of importance and takes pains to regulate the future, always trying to anticipate and avoid some unpleasant eventuality. He is unwilling to place his hand trustfully into his Maker's, leaving the future to providence.

He also likes to worry about the past. It is a part and parcel of "devout" life, this mulling over of past defections. We must dot our i's and cross our t's. We can't trust God to forgive us our sins; we can't believe that in His goodness He has already forgiven us. No, we must do it all ourselves. We can rely only on our own efforts, not on the sacrament, not on the power of "I release you from your sin." We dare not accept the truth that He, in His loving care, has given us the light of grace to make a true act of contrition necessary for the worthy reception of the sacrament. It is the pride of man, with his fancies! It can, of course, be a mental sickness, this tendency to worry. But more often it is simply born of pride or destructive self-reliance. Thus, we must earnestly strive to free our minds from useless thoughts and worries.

Finally, there is the cleansing directed at setting us free from moods and ups-and-downs of temperament. Every temperament has its own lights and shades. A sanguine person is very easily moved by pleasant impressions, but these impressions are superficial. He is charming in social intercourse, friendly, not exactly reliable. He is easily exhausted and not one who concentrates or who can be expected to rise to an emergency. The choleric man is equally easily moved, but in his case impressions go deep and are enduring. He is more accessible to serious ideas than to superficial impressions. He is a man of energy, endurance, initiative, and strong will; but he has a tendency to pride, to tyranny, to aggressiveness. The melancholy man is slow and easily hurt. He is open to depressing ideas; slow, patient, enduring, more contemplative than active. Then there is the man of phleg-matic character. Not easily moved, he is one on whom noth-ing makes a very deep or lasting impression. Practically nothing ever upsets his equilibrium. It is easy for him to for-give and forget. But he prefers a middle course and is seldom moved to any heroic decision or any great work.

It is obviously no easy matter for a man to remake his whole nature, strengthening his good parts so that they may bear fruit and uprooting his undesirable tendencies. Not even all the saints honored on our altars were successful in overcoming all the faults of their characters. But they did strive tirelessly to rid themselves of temperamental flaws. Do not even worldlings strive to master their weaknesses? What a guard they have to keep on their temperament in or-der to maintain their ascendancy over their fellow men, to gain esteem, to emerge triumphant in the battle for exist-ence! "For the children of this world are wiser in their gen-eration than the children of light" (Lk 16: 8). Can we afford to lag behind the children of the world if we desire to share God's life with Him?

★　★　★

THE FIRST decisive step in a life of Christian sanctity is the cleansing of the heart. Cleansing from sin and conscious un-truth, from undesirable habits, from self-seeking, from thinking only in terms of natural man, from useless preoccu-pation with worry, faults of character and temperament. . . . Guarding it against every sin and every conscious perver-sion. . . . The labor of a lifetime!

Can we possibly accomplish this task?—Certainly not of ourselves alone. We must turn to God. "Create in me, O Lord, a clean heart." Relying upon strength and grace, with our eyes fixed upon the loving Lord who desires to live His pure, holy life in us, we can go confidently to work. "I can do all things through Christ which strengtheneth me" (Phil 4: 13).

We must examine ourselves carefully to discover if, in the past, we have tackled the task of cleansing the heart seriously enough.

Our decision stands firm: To live God's life with Him in Christ Jesus, to the pattern set by Jesus and strengthened by His power working in us. "He that abideth in me, and I in him [as the vine and the branches], the same beareth much fruit. For without me ye can do nothing."

5. *Sin*

For I know my iniquity and my sin is always before me.
PSALM 50: 51

"HE CHOSE us in him before the foundation of the world, that we should be holy and unspotted in his sight" (Eph 1: 4), as copartners in the divine life. Daily we should renew the undertaking to possess it more completely and live it more perfectly till we reach perfection in the presence of God. There "we shall be like to him, because we shall see him as he is; and every one that hath this hope in him sanctifieth himself, as he also is holy" (Jn 3: 2–3). It is in Baptism that this light first dawns upon the soul. After Baptism, the Church gives us a white dress, the symbol of the glory extended to us, with the words "Receive this white dress and wear it unspotted, even to the judgment seat of God." Let us consider the gift of God we received in Baptism and examine ourselves to discover to what extent we have worn the white dress unstained. "I acknowledge my transgressions, and my sin is ever before me."

I. WE HAVE SINNED

We should carry the white dress, the divinely beautiful garment of God's child, unspotted through life. Do we?—Well, for a few years, yes. Those were the days of childhood. But scarcely do we enter years of discretion, in which we distinguished good from evil, when sin begins to steal into the paradise of the young heart: small sins, bigger sins, mortal sins. We have greatly sinned. We all have reason to pray incessantly: "Forgive us our trespasses." "Have mercy on me, O Lord, according to thy great mercy, . . . and blot out my ini-

quity. . . . To thee only have I sinned" (Ps 50: 1–4). We become like the prodigal who wandered into a far country "and
there wasted his substance, living riotously. And after he had
spent it all, there came a mighty famine in that country; and
he began to be in want. . . . And returning to himself he said:
I will arise, and will go to my father, and say unto him: 'Father, I have sinned against Heaven, and before thee'" (Lk
15: 12–19).

Father, I have sinned in thought, in desires, in words, in
deeds and omissions. I have sinned against God, against my
neighbor, and against myself. I have sinned against the commandments of God, against the duties of my rank and calling. I have sinned in the seven deadly sins. I have drawn
others into sin with me, caused them annoyance, led them
into temptation, and given them incentive to sin. I have
committed many grievous sins. I have committed venial sins
in faults of negligence and omission, some more, some less
deliberate; sins every day of my life for many years. "Sins
more numerous than the hairs of my head" (Ps 39: 13).

All this persists despite the many aids given us to keep our
baptismal robe unspotted; despite the directions and teachings we receive in our home, at school, in church; despite the
many inspirations, intuitions, warnings of our inner grace;
despite the many good examples illuminating our path; despite contemplation, retreats, spiritual exercises, confessions,
and good resolutions; despite daily attendance at Mass and
daily Communion; despite the good books we read, the
many prayers we say. Priests and religious do well to remind
themselves especially of the grace of priesthood and of the
religious life, with its powerful aids—sacred vows and clois-
ter discipline. "Father, I have sinned against Heaven and
against thee. I am not worthy to be called thy son."

"Have mercy on me, O God, according to thy great
mercy; and according to . . . thy tender mercies blot out my
iniquity. Wash me yet more from my iniquity, and cleanse
me from my sin. For I know my iniquity, and my sin is always

before me. . . . Thou shalt sprinkle me with hyssop, and I shall be cleansed; thou shalt wash me, and I shall be made whiter than snow" (Ps 50: 3–7).

Just as the wanderer tramping along the highway is bound to collect dust, we are unable to avoid daily contamination with the dust of sin. "There is nothing in which I can find honor, but much that obliges me to humble myself to the dust, for I am weak and frail to the innermost core of my being" (*The Imitation of Christ*). *Mea culpa, mea culpa, mea maxima culpa. . . .*

2. WHAT SIN INVOLVES

"Who can understand sin?" asks the Psalmist. In order to appreciate sin, we must first understand what God is. For sin is the negation of God: an attack upon His very nature, on His love and wholeness; a violation of the inalienable rights of the Almighty. It separates us from God, from life, and thrusts us as deeply into the pit of destruction as our divine life lifts and exalts us.

So sin in the first place touches God; it is an insult to God. "I am the Lord, thy God." We have to relate everything to God, serving Him and living for Him. We commit sins; and when we do, what happens? We really relate all things to ourselves, to the satisfaction of our own passion, whether it is pride or sensuality. The faculties of our body and soul are given to us in order that we may serve God with them. Instead, we divert them to our own purposes in defiance of God's commandments and will. We unjustly seize upon the things that serve us and that belong to God, asking by their very nature nothing but to serve God—and force them to our own ends, against God's will and purpose. We seek our own honor instead of God's honor, our own will instead of God's will. We set ourselves against God, above God: ourselves in the first place; God—where?

We identify ourselves with God to His disadvantage, reducing Him to the level of an idol—the idol of our own ego, of money, of success, of ambition, of honor, of lust, of unbridled passion, of love, of friendship. We prefer a created thing to God Himself, in effect raising this idol above Him, saying to it: "You are my all, my God. I live for you." Is not this an offense against God? An insult to God?

Sin is disobedience to God, conscious transgression against His commandments. "I am the Lord." God has the right to command. His commandments are norm and law. We sin. In doing so, we throw to the winds the obedience we owe Him. The will, the commandments of God, are nothing to us. We trample His laws underfoot and go our way; this, after dedicating ourselves to His service in Baptism! This is all our vow amounts to—a broken word in which we are dishonored.

Sin is ingratitude to God. By His love He has delivered us from eternal damnation. He has made us His beloved children in Christ. He has sown so much good seed in the soil of our souls. Yet we sin. We do not take advantage of the gifts of nature or our supernatural gifts and the sacraments, of our Christianity or our membership in religious orders; frequently, we misuse them. Instead of honoring God with our spirit and our body, living for Him and fulfilling His holy will, we range ourselves against Him in disobedience and wrongdoing, to His offense and dishonor. "He planted [his vineyard] with choicest vines, . . . and looked that it should bring forth grapes, and it brought forth wild grapes. . . . What is there that I ought to do more to my vineyard, that I have not done to it? Was it that I looked that it should bring forth grapes, and it hath brought forth wild grapes?" (Is 5: 2–4).

All sin is against Christ, our Lord and Redeemer. In order to save us from sin and destruction, the Son of God came down to earth and dwelt among us. He came "to save that which was lost" (Mt 18: 11). How much must He have loved us! What did it cost Him to save us? What message for us have the sorrowful mysteries of the Rosary, the Stations of the Cross, the crucifix, the nails, the lance, the corpse in the lap of the Mother? All this is for us—suffered for every one of us. All this simply to bestow upon us the grace of being God's children, with all the accompanying graces we require.

We sin. What does the price He paid matter to us? That was His most bitter reflection on the Mount of Olives. With divine clarity He foresaw all our ingratitude. "My people, what have I done to you? Wherein have I caused you sadness? Answer me. Because I brought you out of Egypt [Baptism], you kept the cross in readiness for me. Because I led you out of the desert and fed you with manna [Holy Eucharist], because I led you to the land of plenty [the Church], you crucified me. It was I who raised you with great might [to the honor of a child of God, copartner in the life of God], and for this you nailed me on the cross. Wherein have I offended you? Answer me" (*Good Friday Improperium*). What answer can we give? Yes, we have requited His love, not with love in return, but with base ingratitude; and ingratitude hurts.

To sin is to render unfruitful His work of redemption in us. Sin hinders the germination and growth of the seeds of grace in our soul; mortal sin, but venial sin, too. Certainly, as long as we only commit venial sins we are on the way to God; but we are handicapped by the many little infidelities and failings. Our inner life cannot prosper while they choke it. The divine graces cannot expand. We put insurmountable obstacles in the way of the redemption and healing that God wishes to perfect in us through the sacraments. When we obstinately ignore these little sins we are the stony ground in which the good seed simply cannot take root. Thus we make the work of redemption unfruitful not only in ourselves but also in others. Can this be otherwise than painful to God?

Sin hurts us too. It is the greatest evil that can come upon us. We have been admitted to copartnership in God's life. If we commit a mortal sin, we cease to have divine life in us.

From divine life we are plunged into the lowest pit of darkness. So far as we are concerned, we have cut ourselves off and excluded ourselves from God's life. We are no longer children of God. We are children of wrath, abominations in the sight of God. We are no longer living branches of Christ, the vine, but withered branches. It remains only for death to sever the last fibers that unite us to the Vine, then we are cast for evermore into the darkness where there is wailing and gnashing of teeth. God, who in Christ loved us so deeply, is obliged to thrust us from Him. That is what sin does for us: lose God, lose all.

Sin carries in itself its own punishment, the pangs of remorse, which pursue the sinner day and night. Often, also, he loses his health, his prosperity, his honor, his good name. Always the burning question persists: How will this end? Unless he returns to the Father, his misfortunes are bound to be increased by the perversion of his conscience, the blinding of his spirit, the relaxation of his willpower, the hardening of his heart; in short, the complete debasement of his character, loss of self-esteem. With all this comes the constant dread of death. That is the hard way of sin here on earth. It can only end, unless God in His mercy intervenes, in definitely cutting him off from God and His life. In everlasting Hell, he is separated from God, separated from happiness and all joy; one misery, hatred, bitterness for all eternity.

Sin extends its influence beyond the individual to the family, the parish, the church, one's country; to mankind in general. Every sin damages the whole. It withdraws the blessing of God from the sinner and at the same time from everyone else; for we are all one body, one complete organism in grace. If one limb is diseased, the whole body necessarily suffers. If one branch is unfruitful, the whole vine bears a diminished crop. If one limb rests under the curse of God, the whole body suffers under that curse. No one can live for himself alone. All this is apart from the scandal with which sin is almost inevitably bound up.

★ ★ ★

WE HAVE sinned. We have sinned exceedingly: inwardly, in thoughts, lusts, wishes, impulses of pride, sensuality, self-love, envy, jealousy, the belittling of others; outwardly, in speech, in commission and omission—we, who have been called to live God's life with Him in Christ Jesus! We have wronged God, Christ the Savior, ourselves, the community.

"I acknowledge my trespass and my sin is ever before me." We regret that we have failed. We examine ourselves carefully and arise renewed to the blessed task that has been imposed upon us. "Regard yourselves as such who, being dead to sin, are alive to God in Christ Jesus, our Lord."

6. *Venial Sin*

Deliver us from evil.

To LIVE God's life with Him means to be cleansed from all sin; from mortal sin to venial sin.

Venial sin, like mortal sin, is a surrender to the ungoverned senses of mortal man. It is, of course, not sufficiently serious to cut us off completely from God. We remain God's children, children of grace, living branches of Christ, the vine. But our copartnership in the life of God, our "being in Christ Jesus," is weakened, loosened. As long as we have such sins on our soul, we fall far behind that high destiny to which God in His love has called and chosen us.

Venial sin is just the kind of sin that suits the pious, in the world and in the convent. These folk are so terrified of mortal sin that venial sin seems to them less dangerous. But for that very reason venial sin is an even greater danger to them. They look upon venial sin as being insignificant and unimportant, and at best they do not abhor it as it deserves. That is unfortunate, for progress and retrogression in spiritual life depend very much on the attitude we adopt toward venial sin. Really to share the life of God, to devote our entire life to God, we must lead a life of perfect love; and this is unthinkable if we regard venial sin as of no account, a thing about which we can make our minds quite easy. "He that is faithful in that which is least is faithful also in much; he that is unjust in the least is unjust also in much" (Lk 16: 10).

I. FORMS OF VENIAL SIN

There is one very insidious way of thinking about venial sin. It betrays itself with the thought or comment "Oh, it's only a venial sin"; for instance, a small "white" lie, a small breach of brotherly love, or a little disobedience to our elders and superiors. These might seem quite negligible until they are recognized as a deliberate trespass against the commandment of God. Of course, venial sin is not a complete turning away from God. We still keep our direction Godward and remain on the right road, but we set our own will above the known will of God and the Savior. Any human desire, any source of enjoyment, that places our earthly satisfaction above God's will is an affront to Him. In giving way to any such satisfaction we turn our backs on the invitation of divine grace. If, instead of following our own will, we had welcomed this invitation, we should have received in reward a new grace and at the same time advanced our progress toward divine love and eternal happiness.

Deliberate venial sin hinders the growth of grace and divine love in us, delaying our reward in Heaven: that is its fruit. A barrier arises in the soul between us and the inflow of God's grace, and this in turn leads to a negligent attitude—an open door to other sins. Our will forms the habit of yielding. Our judgment becomes clouded. Our faith weakens. Natural desires reawaken; our zeal diminishes. The ideal of God's love vanishes more and more from our vision. We are overcome with fatigue; we lose our joy and courage.

The mischief is completed when venial sin becomes habitual. Many pious people are almost constantly bad tempered, unfaithful, inexact in small matters. They are impatient, unloving in their thoughts, words, and judgments; unguarded in speech and given to selfishness; loose and indolent in religious matters; ungoverned, too talkative. They treat the reputations of others lightly, are not scrupulously honest, not sufficiently kind, and more. They know their faults and shortcomings. No doubt they are deeply contrite about them in confession. But their sorrow does not go deep enough, and they do not seize upon the means whereby they could uproot their sins. They do not regard each of these sins for what it really is, a millstone around their necks, which is dragging them down. They cannot see how rapidly they are slipping back into the natural state, allowing themselves to be actuated entirely by human thoughts and human motives to the complete disregard of the promptings of divine grace within. They misuse the grace of God, and their soul pays the price in the gradual dimming of its God-given glory. It cannot reestablish its former relation with God; He seems no longer the beloved and loving Father to whom the soul can turn with childlike tenderness. Something has come between the soul and God. Indeed, it cannot be otherwise.

Are we not behaving badly toward God and the Savior with our habitual venial sins—turning to the things He abominates and thereby laying ourselves open to the danger of being separated from Him forever? This kind of behavior neutralizes the help of grace. It reduces us more and more to the state of indifference and lukewarmness and augments our blindness, our self-sufficiency, and our pride. How can we wonder that this state of affairs widens the breach between ourselves and God? The ruination of the soul can be traced to the multitude of habitual venial sins. That is the usual history of the soul's downfall.

The so-called semivoluntary venial sins are in a different class altogether. There are many devout people who have such a horror of venial sin that it is impossible for them willingly to commit one—even the smallest—with eyes wide open. At the same time, these people are necessarily constantly aware of certain faults causing them much humiliation, and sometimes anger and annoyance to others. This, despite all good resolutions, despite every effort on the sinner's part to avoid them. These are not intentional sins, but semivoluntary, in character. In a wider sense, they may be said to spring from weakness.

Semivoluntary sins are of three kinds; first, the so-called sins of haste. They are due to absentmindedness, often caused by an easy-going temperament that has become habitual or by sheer rashness. A decision is made without a moment's consideration as to whether it is sinful or not. Another form of venial transgression is the sin of surprise. In certain situations, such as an emergency, a sudden upset, a nervous impulse may precipitate us into an act of disobedience to God, whether we approve or not. We give way to the pressure of the situation and the harm is done, even though we may not have brought it on ourselves by the full clarity of conscious desire. Then there are sins of weakness in the narrower sense of the word—nervous agitations causing loss of patience, resolution, and willpower. We have the sensation afterward of having failed in courage to control ourselves, of not having fought sufficiently hard to retain our gentleness, love, and calm judgment when we felt them threatened by excitement, even though we cannot determine exactly whether we transgressed against them of our own free will.

These semivoluntary faults, however, are really sins; and that is why we should regard them as serious menaces and do everything in our power to avoid them. Of course, we know perfectly well that we can never escape them altogether. The Church teaches that it is impossible for any human being to remain entirely free of venial sin except in a case of extraordinary grace, like that, for instance, of the Blessed Virgin Mary (Council of Trent, 6th sess., Can. 23). Our aim in the fight against these half-voluntary sins is not so much their complete elimination at all price as their reduction and suppression, so far as lies in our power. This should be our program: never consciously and deliberately to commit a premeditated venial sin and to avoid the semivoluntary sins and failings as much as possible.

2. HOW CAN WE COMBAT VENIAL SIN?

The answer to this crucial question depends chiefly on the attitude we adopt toward venial sin. Deliberate venial sins, the occasional as well as the habitual, must be got rid of at all costs. Until we have given up these sins, complete unity with God, perfect love, is impossible.

Semivoluntary venial sins are another matter. Naturally, they must be regarded with abhorrence because they trespass against God's commandments. No sooner do we become aware of having fallen into them than we are overcome with a sense of guilt and remorse. We humble ourselves for having spoken or acted thoughtlessly, for having made an irrational decision in an emergency, for having weakened in the face of emotion or annoyance. We come to God and beg His forgiveness. We renew our determination to be more watchful and courageous. We pray for grace not to fall again. In short, we *can* use these semivoluntary sins as a means to greater self-knowledge and self-abasement, as a driving force bringing us more often to God and our Savior, to acts of penance and renewed resolution to combat evil. Hence it is that these semivoluntary venial sins, instead of being disadvantageous or discouraging to our progress, may actually spur us on to greater purity and fervor. They can be an aid on the way to God, an actual grace. We must never, however, give up the struggle to restrain and diminish them. But how? What means can we adopt to this end?

First of all, we can turn to prayer. Human wish and will alone cannot suffice. "For it is God who worketh in you both to will and to accomplish, according to his goodwill" (Phil 2: 13). Even the desire to remain free from sin is not in the first instance our own work. It is created in us by the working of inner grace (Council of Orange [A.D. 529], Can. 4). God's grace must enlighten us to acquire a deeper understanding of what venial sin is and what it means. God's grace must give us the courage and strength to fight against it in all its forms day by day, our whole life long, with inviolable fidelity and zeal. Grace, however, is given to those who ask for it. "Ask and it shall be given you" (Lk 11: 9).

In the second place, it is a matter of adopting good principles in regard to the so-called "small" things—rules, directions, duties, and so on. In reality we can afford to regard nothing as small. In every duty, every obligation, every wish, will, or command of our proper superiors, in everything of good or evil that the day brings forth, the eye of faith must perceive God, the Savior, God's providence, God's will, God's pleasure. If we live by faith, even the things that seem small from the human viewpoint become important, holy, and awesome. We recognize and comprehend in small things the holy will of God and God Himself. Thus it becomes easy for us to guard against every form of neglect and disloyalty.

It is of the highest importance to have a right idea of the significance of venial sin, especially the deliberate variety. To look upon venial sin as something negligible is the beginning of the end. We must possess the unshakable conviction that venial sin is an insult to God, a thing God hates and abominates with His strength and His holiness. Venial sin is disobedience to God's commandments; it involves ingratitude to Him who loves us unendingly and gives us all the good there is. After mortal sin, it is the greatest evil that can befall us, worse than death or the loss of worldly goods or man's esteem. Even if it does not separate us from God, even if it does not rob us of God's presence in our soul, of our sonship to God, still it retards our growth in divine life, in sanctifying grace, and supernatural virtue. It militates against grace and forces it back so that it cannot be quickened into action. The seed of divine life, which is sown in our souls, cannot flourish while poison weeds spring up side by side with it. They spoil the earth and infect the atmosphere. So long as we are not convinced of the destructive power of venial sin in our souls and God's displeasure over it, we will too readily regard it as a thing of no importance; and that means we will never overcome it.

The sacrament of Penance is another effective aid in combating venial sin. Regular confession not only insures forgiveness of past sins but gives us strength for future effort, by means of repentance, absolution, and the penance the priest imposes upon us. It reduces the tendency to relapse, increases our leaning toward good, and entitles us to renewed grace with which to resist venial sin and avoid it. Much depends, however, upon the genuine repentance with which we approach the sacrament and how much honest, practical resolution we bring to it. Unfortunately, very often we do not draw as much benefit from the sacrament as we should.

A powerful aid is constant watchfulness over our outer senses, over our thoughts and fancies, over our wishes, desires, attractions, affections, and habits. "Watch ye, and pray that ye enter not into temptation" (Mt 26: 41)—that you may guard yourself against temptation and sin. Without watchfulness and the control of the senses—over gluttony, the tongue, moodiness, and revenge, of contention, pride, criticism, and the belittling of others—it is impossible to gain ascendancy over venial sin. We pray for victory over venial sin, and it is well that we should. We meditate and reflect, we receive the sacraments, we endeavor to follow the example of the saints. But in spite of all these helps, not to mention the many graces we have received, we still retain the habit of venial sin and commit it without full knowledge and consent. What is lacking?—Watchfulness and self-denial. Mortification must accompany prayer. "Watch and pray." Again, "This kind [of devil] can go out [be destroyed] by nothing but by prayer and fasting" (Mk 9: 28).

Fostering a spirit of contrition is also a powerful help. This is the spirit habitual to the prodigal son after he has returned to his father. The father forgives him and takes him once again to his heart. But in the heart of the son there remains forever a feeling of remorse that he offended the father and a longing to please the father with increased loyalty, thus making good the fault he committed while regaining the life he had lost. This feeling of repentance, this sense of enduring regret for past sins and gratitude toward the good, forgiving Father prompts us to pray again and again for pardon: "Forgive us our trespasses." This spirit of contrition puts us always on our guard, so that old habits may not reemerge or the enemy, feigning death, steal in upon us while we sleep. It puts us on our guard so that we may overcome our passions and perverted desires and resolutely withstand temptation, by forcing us to remain constantly in a state of prayer against sin.

The essential thing is to keep our hearts aglow with love for our Lord and Savior. Where love glows, virtue will also flourish, together with a firm resolution to combat venial sin. The question of inner growth and the soul's purity is above all a question of love's growth. As we love, venial sin will vanish, almost of its own accord. We seldom take the right attitude toward venial sin. We plant so many signposts along the road, put so many obstacles in life's pathway, that we actually create bottlenecks, making it impossible to march directly, freely, and joyfully toward the height of salvation. Our way is beset with a thousand notices, a thousand interdictions: "This is sinful," "Dare I risk it?" and the like. All this is so negative. But love simplifies all this. With love, the task is as good as done. Loves gives us strength to make the necessary sacrifices, to offer up the necessary renunciations, joyfully to reject this and that, returning a decisive *No* to all the many promptings of self-love and keeping alive the alertness necessary to prevent ourselves from falling into even the smallest transgression.

Out of love must grow a detestation of all the venial sins that accompany us unconsciously through life and are so deeply rooted in our natures that their influence helps to determine our whole outlook. Love can save us from the crippling effects of fearing sin excessively; from uncertainty and overscrupulous diffidence toward the many possibilities and opportunities of committing venial sin. It binds us to God, to Christ, and therefore gives us definite guidance. It drives us toward good, toward perfect good, in spite of all difficulties. It does not stop at fulfilling duties, obeying commands: even fear would do that much. Love is high above duty; it does far more, gives far more than mere duty demands. Love gives the soul strength to exercise perpetual watchfulness, to take all necessary precautions, to overcome all obstacles, to avoid everything that might displease God, the Savior. That is love's goal. A goal far higher than that of merely avoiding sin.

Love is a power greater than any other power. Love transforms the one who loves, gives him new, constructive ideas, gives him impulse and motive, endows him with previously unimagined strength. It is certainly no easy matter to avoid venial sin in the stress and turmoil of this world. It involves nothing less than bringing our resistance to such a pitch of efficiency that it almost automatically keeps us to the right path, making any deviation impossible. But for this our soul must be tuned in to higher inspiration—an inspiration that can spring only from a burning love of God, our Savior.

★   ★   ★

"He who is negligent in small things gradually comes to ruin"; slow but sure.

Our task is to live the holy life of God with Him. That means continual combat against sin, venial sin no less than mortal.

Our program is clear and definite. Every intentional venial sin must be ruled out. Furthermore, an equal vigilance must be extended to the semivoluntary venial sins in order to repress and starve them.

The means to this end have been given to us. We only need to use them. Here they are again: prayer, right principles in regard to small things and venial sins, devout and constant reception of the sacrament of Penance, watchfulness, and, above all, love. For this is "the culmination of the law" (Rom 13: 10).

Let us examine ourselves. What does venial sin mean to me? What has been my opinion of it in the past? What has been my attitude toward it in the practical affairs of daily life? What must I do or leave undone? What can I improve?

The fundamental truth is that the ruin of countless souls can be traced to venial sin that was not taken seriously.

7. *The Enemy*

All seek the things that are their own.
PHILIPPIANS 2: 21

IT IS NO small matter to be called to participate in the divine life, to be a branch of Christ, the vine, receiving the inflow of His divine nature until we can say, "I live, but not I; Christ lives in me." He desires to live in us; it is a necessity of His divine nature to identify Himself with the soul inhabiting us and determining our thoughts, our will, our actions. With His spirit He desires to fill our lives; and in this He is constantly opposed by the enemy that disputes His sovereignty over us. This enemy is not so much Satan, not so much the world; it is the enemy in ourselves—the enemy who was born when we were born and who, even before we attain the full use of reason, gets us into his clutches. He retains his hold on us through our passions, through the dimness of our understanding, through our weak will and our sins, evil inclinations, bad habits; and his power over us increases daily. This enemy boasts of his conquests even when we have wrung victory from him; finds nourishment even in our virtues, being fed and strengthened by our failings. This enemy rises with us in the morning and stands all day by our side, watching for a chance to do us harm, poisoning and belittling all that we do and leave undone.

This enemy is self-love. This is the enemy we must fight. If we conquer it, then the sovereignty of Christ is assured. Then indeed "Not I, but Christ, liveth in me" (Gal 2: 20).

I. SELF-LOVE: WHAT IT IS

We meet self-love every day, at every turn, in a thousand guises, always externally prosperous, well-dressed, versatile, charming, polished, full of seduction and persuasive art, full of sophistication, lies, and sham.

Self-love is the driving force in the bustle of daily life. "All seek the things that are their own," complains the apostle Paul (Phil 2: 21): self, personal profit, personal interest, egotism, selfishness. Self-love is the deep, secret root of vice and sins that are incessantly driving mankind to destruction: laziness, weakness of character, disloyalty, treachery, untruth, greediness, avarice, and the sins of the flesh and spirit. Self-love is the mother of all crime and wrongdoing among mankind—of historic injustices that cry to Heaven, of tyranny, uncharitableness, of wars, the destruction of our own happiness and that of others. It is self-love that tears faith and religion out of people's hearts and robs millions of their hope of Heaven.

Side by side with the pursuit of self there is an even more refined variety of self-love—that of the pious: a "spiritual" self-love. This, too, one meets daily in the hearts, thoughts, impulses, words, and actions of the pious.

The soul, shall we say, ardently desires virtue and perfection. But behind all the zeal there is a secret desire to be admired, to amount to something, to glory in one's perfection, to marvel at oneself with secret pride.

The soul does its best to fly from sin. But self-love creeps subtly in. The soul becomes confused, then, seeking to avoid it not so much because it is an insult to God but because it might cloud the soul's beauty. Or it may adopt an attitude of "superiority" to such weaknesses.

Self-love demands revelations and compensations, particularly showy graces and gifts. It likes to compare its own gifts with those of others, inclining to envy and jealousy.

Self-love misleads the soul as to the actual goal of spiritual zeal. Instead of recognizing this simply as God's will in all and above all, it begins to look upon the improvement of life conditions and personal perfection as the main things to strive for. This false aim then perverts our motives. The soul tends to attach itself to schools of thought and "improvement" of its own choosing, never guessing that its anxiety for self-improvement is a delusion and another form of self-glorification.

Self-love puts the soul into a pother about its sins and failings. It becomes depressed and cast down by its petty inhibitions and limitations. It begins to hate the sight of its own insignificance and gets so impatient with the slow working of God and His grace that it becomes discontented. Hadn't it formed a totally different opinion of its own powers, regarding grace as a sort of magic? The slowness of God gets on its nerves.

Self-love is fond of setting the soul too high a target. It keeps the example of Christ and the saints in view, vaingloriously aiming to imitate these patterns. Hasn't it done its best? But it simply cannot grasp why it falls short of what it sees in Christ and the saints. Then it gets discouraged.

Self-love keeps its own good deeds constantly in sight: the conscientiousness with which the soul fulfills its duties, the zeal with which it enters into prayer and pious practices. Soon the incense of self-praise swells the soul with pride.

Self-love agitates the soul, makes it impatient and discontented when it encounters disturbance, wandering thoughts, interrupted concentration, and temptations in its prayers, or when the glow of satisfaction fails to follow them, when spells of weakness and impotence set in, or spiritual aridity and rebellion against prayer occur.

Self-love leads to touchiness and impatience with our fellow man. It makes us unyielding, angry, aggressive in stressing our own personality and our own rights. It makes us cold and indifferent, reserved, unjust in judgment and speech about our neighbor. Self-love delights in dwelling upon its own experiences, inspirations, difficulties, and sufferings. Self-love likes to compare its own doings and its own piety with those of others, watching them and pronouncing judgment upon them. It gives others no credit, sees only their faults, but vaunts itself in comparison and attributes evil intentions to them, sometimes even wishing them ill. In spite of all our piety, self-love lays us wide open to being easily wounded. We are put out, repelled, offended, when we are not taken sufficiently seriously or made as much of as we expected.

It is impossible to enumerate here all the forms that spiritual self-love can take. We shall merely indicate the forms it can assume in the community life of the convent. There it often masquerades as reserve, or it may manifest itself in the trick of obtaining some slight advantage over the rest of the community. It can be traced in the ultra-punctilious observance of rules and regulations, inclining a person to spy on others or to assume an officious control, to be unloving and critical of superiors, complaining that they are slack or too lenient. Self-love often identifies itself with self-will, hindering us from giving our loyalty blindly or performing what we are required to do without question. Self-love leads us to faultfinding, bad temper, discontent, or want of charity toward our superiors and other members of the order.

Self-love, moreover, is the source of all disturbances, excitements, panics, disappointments, unfulfilled wishes, expectations, plans, resolutions, and intentions—everything that keeps the soul in suspense, robbing it of inner peace, of concentration and the true spirit of prayer. Therefore it is robbed of complete unity with God.

From the foregoing, the decisive part self-love plays in a life of piety is clear. Deep down, self-love is the fundamental cause of all our sins. What is sin? A purely temporal, fleeting satisfaction gained by uncontrolled surrender to some vanity, craziness—to some idol. All this yielding can be traced to perverted self-love. The serpent steals into paradise. "Ye shall not die; ye shall be as gods" (Gen 3: 4). With these words the evil one appealed to the self-love of Eve, who allowed herself to be bemused, reached for the forbidden fruit and shared it with Adam. Since then the torrent of sin has flown over mankind, thrusting its way into homes, into hearts, into thoughts and desires, into the will, the bodies, the speech, actions, and transactions of men. All this is the fruit of self-love. Self-love turned Cain into a fratricide, the apostle into the betrayer of our Lord. Is there anything more pernicious than self-love?

Self-love is the enemy of God in us. We are created to love God. For the same reason we have been made one with Christ. The inestimable riches and graces of Christianity have been made accessible to us. "Thou shalt love the Lord thy God" (Mt 22: 37). "He that loveth not abideth in death" (1 Jn 3: 14). But who truly loves God? It is he who gives himself wholly, without reserve, to pleasing God and doing His divine will; he who seeks nothing for himself but lives only for the honor, the service, and the glory of God. Self-love? It simply loves itself, not God. Self-love is the direct opposite to the love of God. Place them both together on a pair of scales and instantly one will go up, the other down. Only when self-love has been supernaturalized can the paradise of divine love dawn upon the soul.

If self-love militates against the love of God, it is necessarily also the enemy of brotherly love. The love of God unifies; self-love causes dissension. Self-love is the great trouble maker, the enemy that sows hatred, envy, strife, in the hearts of men. It is forever preoccupied with its own advantage, indifferent to the rights of others, to love, or to the commandment of brotherly love. Love, St. Paul writes to the Corinthians, "is patient, is kind; [it] envieth not, is not puffed up; is not ambitious, is not provoked to anger, thinketh no evil" (1 Cor 13: 4–5).

What follows from this?—The truth that every degree of holiness, every kind of perfection, all spiritual growth, depend upon the elimination of self-love. Only from the ruins of self-love can arise the new man in whom Christ lives and rules. A further truth: the only road to perfection is that of cutting oneself adrift from self-love.

2. HOW WE CAN OVERCOME THE ENEMY

We can conquer the enemy through God's work and our own.

(a) Our work falls into two parts: prayer and the gradual atrophying of self-love.

Grace derives from prayer and is inseparably linked with it. "Ask, and it shall be given you; seek, and you shall find" (Mt 7: 7). "Blessed are they that hunger and thirst after justice [holiness]: for they shall have their fill" (Mt 5: 6). The more we pray, earnestly pray, the more we receive grace to starve out self-love. Our prayer must be fundamentally an act of love to God, to Christ. As this divine love grows, self-love automatically diminishes. "Increase in us Thy love."

The pivot of our prayer must rest upon the Mass. Here we participate in the sacrifice that Christ the High Priest Himself offers up. We become one with Him in the offering to the Father. In the sacrifice we surrender all our perverted inclinations and habits, our vain affections and attachments, our own will with all its wishes and excitements: *Suscipe, sancte Pater*—"Accept it, holy Father." To offer up means to renounce, means breaking with our finite personal self in order to belong wholly to God, dedicated to Him and united with Him. As sacrifices, blessed by Almighty God, we leave the altar in the conscious glow of belonging to Him. We have changed; we have only one thing in mind, to lose ourselves completely in our Maker. Here, in the liturgical prayers, participating in Mass and in the grace of Holy Communion, we bury the old Adam with all his selfish impulses. Here the new man, the man in God and Christ-love, is born.

The withering away of sensuality and weakness goes hand-in-hand with prayer. All the lusts of the flesh become atrophied as we constantly and sincerely pray. Prayer gives us the strength to master our inclinations and passions, our pride, our self-deceptions, our excessive self-confidence, our moods, our obstinacy, our loquacity, our indecision, our faulty imagination and memory, and all other failings.

(b) But having done all this, we are still impotent slaves. Our own labors are insufficient. We lack the singleness of vision to master self-love. We lack the brutal courage to tear it out of our system. Here God must step in; and He does.

He takes chisel and hammer in hand and goes to work. He desires to create a masterpiece, the most faithful copy of His beloved, only-begotten Son—a child of God, reproducing His own likeness and reflecting His beauty. All this so that the love He bears toward His children may live again in them as the highest possible perfection.

He steps in. He works on us outwardly through His loving providence, through divine decrees and authority, through the incidents and coincidences of daily life, through the circumstances in which we are placed, through the sicknesses, discouragements, successes and failures, the bitternesses and difficulties that befall us, through the crosses we bear and the sufferings; likewise, through the many joys of our life, both small and great. We may recognize His hand in everything, working for the destruction of our self-love, our enemy.

He also works in us from within. He is the jealous God who will not tolerate in our souls any other God than Himself. He is jealous for the complete surrender of our heart, that we make Him the only goal of our desires and wishes, that we may truly love Him with our whole strength and everything else only for love of Him. He is jealous for the honor we pay Him, in order that our spirit may humble itself and acknowledge Him as all-in-all, blindly yielding our entire consciousness so that we may be completely dependent upon His inspiration; losing our own knowledge, our own understanding, guided by His light and His spirit alone, blindly, trustfully giving ourselves to Him without reserve.

God in His love is so immeasurably jealous that He cannot endure the least trace of self-love in our hearts. He insists on nothing less than the complete annihilation of self.

His work of destruction starts with robbing us of the consolations our heart finds at first in giving itself to Him. These sweet comforts in the early stages have a necessary and valuable part to play, for they dissolve the ties that still link the soul, in its unadvanced state, to earthly things. They are just a foretaste, as it were, and we ourselves are bound to recognize them as such. So it is inevitable that our first love of God should be not entirely pure but slightly tinged with self-love. Gradually, when these first compensations have done their work, God steps in. Step by step, and at intervals, He withdraws this voluptuous comfort from the soul. Periods of aridity set in, coupled with periodical and really burdensome lack of concentration.

We feel none of the ardor that used to accompany our devotions; indeed, prayer may even become irksome. A coolness develops, and we find difficulty in establishing contact with God on the old, easy footing. The soul is conscious of having entered upon a crisis. Happy is he who has the strength to await the passing of this phase with patience, constancy, and humility. If he is loyal, offering God willingly, wholeheartedly, all that is required of him, he will begin to love God for His own sake and not for the sake of His sweetness and His gifts.

Now we are ready to enter upon the second stage of God's war against self-love. After the periods of consolation and aridity have alternated for some time, God withdraws all feeling from the tested soul, so that the bliss of conscious awareness of God is experienced rarely and only for brief moments. In this process the soul begins to become simpler, more pure. It is no longer conscious of being loved or of loving. Yet at the same time it loves more deeply and purely than it ever did before. It loves regardless of itself. It forgets itself completely. Its consciousness of loving no longer depends upon emotion, as it once did, but upon the fact that it has become more steadfast, loyal, patient, enduring, kinder, less selfish, firmer in resisting temptation, and altogether more dependable. Zeal and fervor have given place to stronger willpower; self has been pushed a good way back. The soul has learned to forget itself and lose itself in God.

We are now at the third stage—the stage of great purification. This is the stage of which St. Catherine of Genoa writes: "Divine love ruins everything that you love. It sends death, sickness, poverty, hatred, strife, calumny, annoyance, untruth, loss of favor with relatives, friends, even with yourself; you know not which way to turn since you derive only shame and misery from all that you once loved. And you cannot understand why divine love should react in this way, as by all human standards it seems unreasonable. And after divine love has kept you for some time thus in the grip of despair, producing a revulsion against all that you formerly loved, suddenly it reveals its own glory. As soon as the soul, naked and forlorn, beholds this, it throws itself without reserve into the arms of God."

The first step in the cleansing of the soul takes the form of great temptation, putting every virtue to the test: temptations against purity, against brotherly love, against trust in God; temptations to anger, to bitterness, to blasphemy, to quarrelling with God. There is a resurrection of all the vices we thought we had conquered. But the soul retains its purity and firmness. It recognizes its frailty, its nothingness. At last it ceases to marvel at itself, to love itself. It recognizes how sinful and how ugly it is and begins to hate and belittle itself. Divine love is at work in the soul.

The second step comes about through much outward humiliation. Calumny is heaped upon the soul. Others withdraw their good opinion; there is talk of hypocrisy; one's words and actions are misunderstood; former friends fall away, forsaking and avoiding us. Even superiors become estranged, withdrawing their former confidence in us. The soul suffers silently, submits to judgment, to calumny, to suspicion, praying with the crucified One: "Father, forgive them!" The soul cannot accuse itself of any of the faults with which it is credited; nevertheless, it bows down in guilt and is convinced that it merits the treatment it receives. God is at work. Self-love must be deprived of every single prop, either from the examination of its own conscience or the good opinion of others.

Still God is not satisfied. The soul could still draw some comfort from leaning upon God, but even this last refuge is withdrawn. In demanding the soul's submission to the semblance of sin, to the great humiliations of mankind, God is both stern and unrelenting; He seems to forsake the soul. It feels itself damned, rejected, lost in darkness, helpless, frightened, forlorn. It cries: "My God, why hast thou forsaken me?" What can it do? Nothing, except throw itself blindly into the arms of the Father, come what may. "Into Thy hands, O Lord, I commend my spirit." The soul has become humble in the eyes of mankind, in its own eyes. It has nothing left on which it can lean.

Then suddenly it awakens. Self-love has been torn from every fiber of its being. Now it is free and ready for divine love. Now at last God shows His radiant countenance. The soul precipitates itself gratefully into the embrace of the Sacred Heart and acknowledges: "God is love."

★   ★   ★

"He who overcomes self-love has gained victory over all" (St. Alphonsus Liguori). He who overcomes self-love gains all: God, his own soul, inner peace, holiness. The only road to perfection lies through the destruction of self-love.

This is a mighty work, a work too difficult for us of our own power to accomplish. But we need not be afraid. Almighty God lives and works in us. Christ the Lord is beside us, fighting the enemy. He floods us with His spirit, His light, His almighty strength. "I am the vine; ye are the branches." "I can do all things in him who strengtheneth me" (Phil 4: 13).

God's purpose in us is the destruction of self-love. We submit ourselves to His guidance, His creative work with hammer and chisel. "God is love."

8. *The Christian Virtues*

"I LIVE, and you shall live" (Jn 14: 19). Share My life, live in the innermost integration with Me, the stem. Our Christian life is the life of a branch of Christ. Therefore it is a life of union with, and for union with, Christ. It is constant growing into and growing out of Christ. The more completely we grow into Christ, the stem, the more His holy life lives in us, radiating His spirit, His life, His virtue and holiness through our religious life. The more intensive and active our virtue is, the more we identify ourselves with the Stem, the stronger and more powerfully the life of the Stem will flow into the branches, awakening and developing in them a life of Christian virtue.

I. THE MEANING OF A LIFE OF VIRTUE

(a) Christian life is growth, a constant process of progression to higher and higher consciousness, a ceaseless urge toward unity and perfection in God's image. When we have cleansed our heart of sin and error, when with prayer and attrition we have, with the help of God's grace, destroyed self-love in all essentials, the way to enlightenment is open. In the process of purification we have gradually acquired a deeper appreciation of religious truth and supernatural, divine values. We are completely convinced that only one thing is necessary (Lk 10: 42). "What doth it profit a man if he gain the whole world and lose his own soul?" (Mt 16: 26).

We also know, however, that purification from sin and the want of faith is not enough: the road leads on to development in Christian virtue—that is, to illumination. Christ Himself is our example and also our source of strength. We turn to Him as a flower turns to the sun. Our thoughts, our inclinations and wishes, revolve around Him. "Draw me; we will run after thee, to the odor of thy ointments [i.e., Thy virtue and holiness]" (Song 1: 3). We desire to be illuminated by Him, the divine sun, so that we may develop our likeness to Him. For it is to this end that God has created us, predestined "to be made conformable to the image of his son" (Rom 8: 29). Thus, natural progress in the sanctified grace we received in Baptism demands that we should take the road of purification and illumination. After cleansing our soul from sin, intensive and positive application to the work of developing a life of virtue, in conscious imitation of our Lord's life on earth not less than His supernatural virtue in the Holy Eucharist, must be our immediate aim.

(b) "This is my beloved Son, in whom I am well pleased; hear ye him" (Mt 17: 5). With these words the Father emphatically held up to us Christ, His own Son made man, as our pattern and teacher. "Hear ye him." Imitate Him, live His life with Him. Christ is the manifestation of God in human form. When He appears as man, He lives and acts in all things as God lives and is obliged by His nature to act. He is God dwelling among us, showing us how we must live in order to be pleasing to God. Everything He did in His life on earth was perfect and holy, first because of the inner love that governed His actions and then because of the manner in which He lived. Even His least significant act was performed divinely; it was the work of God and therefore completely pleasing to the Father. Hence, all the works of Jesus are an example, a pattern of holiness for us to follow. "I have given you an example, that ye should do as I have done." It is consequently the express will of the Father that we should follow the life of Jesus, yes, actually live as He lived, in imitation of His virtues. It is also the express will of Christ; "Learn of me" (Mt 11: 29). The Apostle says emphatically: "Put ye on the Lord Jesus Christ" (Rom 13: 14). "Be ye like-minded with Jesus"—in the same love, humility, obedience, and esteem of fellow man (Phil 2: 5). We are enjoined to acquire Christ's virtue to such an extent that "not I, but Christ, liveth in me" (Gal 2: 20), lost completely in Christlikeness, a radiation of His spirit and virtue.

(c) The mystery of our living unity with Christ reveals to us the purpose of our striving for virtue. Virtue is the expression, the natural radiation of our "living in Christ." "I am the vine; ye are the branches. He that liveth in me and I in him, the same shall bring forth much fruit [i.e., virtue]." Our virtue is the measure of our life in Christ. It is also the food that nourishes that life. Divorced from conscious effort to acquire virtue and develop it, life in Christ and with Christ is unthinkable. This is the actual meaning of a Christian life: to live Christ's life with Him. A life of virtue is therefore not a matter of entirely free choice but an inescapable duty, which our integration with Christ, through Baptism, imposes upon us. "So do you also reckon that you are dead to sin through Baptism, but alive unto God, in Christ" (Rom 6: 11).

"Live for God." We live for Him to the exact extent to which we live the holy life of Jesus, the stem, in honest striving for virtue and the constant growth of virtue. In striving for humility, for self-denial, for purity, for courage, for surrender to the Father, we, as branches of Christ, the stem, renew and keep alive His humility, self-denial, love, purity, and strength. When the baptized Christian, the branch of Christ, bows in humility, this humility is absorbed in the self-humiliation that Christ the Lord practiced on earth when He was made man, when he was subject to Mary and Joseph, when He washed the apostles' feet. It is His humility, in which He, through us, the branches, worships and glorifies the Father.

Our poverty of spirit attaches itself to the poverty our Lord chose in the crib, in the flight into Egypt, in Nazareth, in His life on earth when He possessed nothing and had no place to lay His head. It is His poverty that He lives again in us, condemning the avarice of the world and honoring the Father. In the whole universe there is only One who honors the Father as He deserves; only One who perfectly prays, who humbles Himself and is completely poor in spirit—Christ. We, however, are an integral part of Him. He continues to live His life of virtue in us, to the glory of the Father. "Stem and branches are so completely one that whatever the one may be, the other is also, nor can they be separated from one another" (St. Augustine, *In Ps.* 40.1). To be a Christian, a branch of Christ, and not to live the virtue of Christ, the stem, is a contradiction. Our unity with Christ, the stem, gives our Christian virtue superior value and priority over all purely natural human virtue. Surely this is sufficient reason for striving with all our might for illumination of virtue.

2. PRIMARY RULES OF A LIFE OF VIRTUE

(a) *The first rule.* Virtue should constantly grow and increase in strength. Supernatural life enters us as a force that awakens powers of the soul, mind, will, and heart to a new realization of God's light of truth and a new urge to live for God, to work for Him, to overcome, to renounce, to suffer everything for love of Him and constantly to aim at holier, more perfect works. A new wave of life floods our being, drawing us with it; a divine power, eliciting ever more energy from the soul and raising our customary existence to an altogether higher level.

It is the nature of the Christian in us to develop and grow. There can be no standing still; whoever ceases to progress, deteriorates. Natural virtue advances toward perfection by character building, learning, courage. It is otherwise with divine Christian virtue. A man may reach a high degree of efficiency and virtuosity through his own willpower, through effort, diligence, and constant practice. Divine virtue, on the other hand, can be given only by God. He raises us from the lower stages of grace and virtue to the high grade; He makes everything clearer with His light and floods us with more divine life than we enjoyed before. We owe our growth in virtue to God and must await it patiently, seeking it from Him.

God gives us three aids in fostering the growth of divine virtue. The first rests upon the sacraments and, in particular, on the Holy Eucharist. The sacraments have the special function of increasing sanctifying grace in us. With this increase the divine virtues automatically grow.

The good works we do are a second aid to growth. Our works cannot of themselves transport us to a higher degree of divine virtue, but they can move Almighty God to increase and strengthen it. Every act of virtue, every good deed, makes us more pleasing to God; and God's satisfaction leads to increase of virtue in us.

The third aid is prayer. "Blessed are they that hunger and thirst after justice [i.e., perfection in virtue]: for they shall have their fill" (Mt 4: 6). Prayer stimulates growth in two ways; by being a good act and, hence, by meriting an increase in the growth of virtue, like any other good deed. Thus, it has a value of its own, a "petition value." "Ask and ye shall receive" (Jn 16: 24). This petition value is increased when we consciously link our lives and our prayers with the community of the Church. We are assured: "For where there are two or three gathered together in my name, there am I in the midst of them" (Mt 18: 20), praying with them.

(b) *The second rule*. Virtue can also decrease; indeed, it can vanish entirely. We are so weak, so inconstant in our will and endeavor, beset by so many difficulties, dangers, enemies.

The greatest enemy of all is venial sin, which is not sufficiently abhorred and not so energetically combated as it should be. Venial sin hinders the growth of grace and virtue, bringing it to a standstill. It cannot attack grace and virtue directly—they are too pure and divine. But it can weaken the flow of life to the branch, thereby retarding the growth of divine virtue, especially love. Venial sins, like dense undergrowth, shut out the light from the tender plants of grace and virtue, gradually choking them. The poisonous roots of habitual venial sins damage the soil, wasting its strength and infecting the atmosphere so that the sun-loving plants of grace and virtue cannot live. At the same time, they destroy many seedlings out of which virtues are destined to grow. That is the pernicious work of venial sin.

Because of mortal sin we may even lose the virtue God has implanted in our soul. For mortal sin primarily kills the most essential of all virtues, love. Once love, which binds us to God, has been killed, all the other virtues (except faith and hope) automatically forsake the soul. The garden of the Christian soul lies waste and desolate, all growth and life destroyed. Only faith remains, a faint glimmer, together with hope, until the poor soul, through unbelief and despair, destroys even these last memories. Then night and barrenness descend. There is left only one pale light, the baptismal imprint (it is not a virtue), which can never be extinguished. It lives on, never ceasing to sigh for the return of grace and virtue.

Which of us is proof against the weakness, the sinfulness, and the wickedness of his heart? "He that himself thinketh to stand, let him take heed lest he fall" (1 Cor 10: 12). "It is not of him that willeth, . . . but of God that showeth mercy" (Rom 9: 16). "With fear and trembling, work out your own salvation" (Phil 2: 12). We can lose grace and virtue. We are all prone to sin and can only thank the mercy and protection of God our Savior if we are spared the loss of grace and virtue.

(c) *The third rule.* All supernatural graces support one another, combine, increase, or decrease together. They do not stand, like so many trees, side by side, each developing in its own fashion. It would be more accurate to say that they constitute one tree, alive with sanctifying grace, in which they have their roots; a single, complete whole. In the human organism an arm does not grow by itself, or a heart or a hand; all parts of the body grow together, fully dependent upon one another. It is exactly the same with the organism of supernatural grace and virtue. All virtues unfold together and increase or decrease by the same impulse.

It cannot be otherwise. All are so closely linked by the virtue of divine love. "Love suffereth long and is kind, envieth not, vaunteth not itself, is not puffed up, is not easily provoked, thinketh no evil; beareth all things, believeth all things, hopeth all things, endureth all things," says the Apostle. He who possesses supernatural love for God and his neighbor is strong and ready to practice every virtue whenever and however opportunity occurs. Love centers all our thinking, our striving, and our dealings on God, regulating our whole life, both private and social, according to the requirements of supernatural Christian virtue.

"Love; then do what you will," says St. Augustine. Whatever springs from perfect love of God is always good, pleasing to God, virtuous. He who has perfect love possesses every virtue: faith, hope, true wisdom, courage, temperance, justice. The more complete the love of God, the simpler and more fruitful our life of virtue. Love is the soul of all virtues. It is therefore most important to strive for love and possess love. All the virtues grow automatically and in pace with love.

It often happens that a person has one virtue and lacks others. He may be chaste but at the same time proud, vain; he may be obedient but also haughty; pious but unloving, self-opinionated, impatient, selfish. That is a disruption of virtues; it springs from the fact that the person concerned is imperfect, weak in virtue. Only where virtue is imperfect and weak do we meet such caricatures of Christian virtue, which, unfortunately, are ubiquitous.

★   ★   ★

THERE IS something magnificent about Christian, super-natural virtue. In this state we truly live the life of Christ with Him. Do we sufficiently appreciate what this means?

How much zeal do I bring to the quest for Christian virtue? To the increase of virtue? To the full realization of Christ in me?

Can I detect in myself any obstacles to the growth of virtue? If so, what must I do?

9. *Temptations*

Lead us not into temptation.
MATTHEW 6: 13

To LIVE the life of Jesus Christ in Him, as members of His body. . . . "He himself hath suffered and been tempted" (Heb 2: 18). The Evangelist reports in detail how our Lord, after His baptism in the Jordan, "was led by the Spirit into the desert, to be tempted by the devil" (Mt 4: 1). Does not this sound mysterious? He, for whom Heaven has just opened on the shores of Jordan, who has been acclaimed by the voice of God: "This is my beloved Son in whom I am well pleased"—is led by the Holy Spirit into the desert of Judea, in order to be tempted by the devil.

The Liturgy of the first Sunday in Lent recognizes in the Lord, who is led into the wilderness to be tempted by the devil, "the whole Christ"—Christ together with His Church, the Mystical Body of Christ, in which we are all included. All of us who have been incorporated into the Church by the sacrament of Baptism are led after Baptism into the wilderness, to live on there, to be tempted, as He was by the devil. We are called upon, as members of Christ's body, endowed with His strength, to conquer the world, the flesh, and the devil for the honor of God, thus securing for ourselves the crown of eternal life. "For he . . . is not crowned, except he strive lawfully" (2 Tim 2: 5). "Blessed is the man that endureth temptation; for when he hath been proved, he shall receive the crown of life" (James 1: 12). "Count it all for joy, when ye shall fall into divers temptations, knowing that the trying of your faith worketh patience" (James 1: 2–3). Tried in temptation, virtue grows and increases in firmness.

I. TEMPTATION: WHAT IT IS

We know all too well from daily experience what temptation is. We suffer from the snares our own nature spread for us, for we have, in consequence of original sin, the spark of greed inherent in our nature. As if greed, the inborn enemy, were not sufficient, others come from outside to entice us with their seductive arts—the world and the devil. "The devil as a roaring lion goes about, seeking whom he may devour" (1 Pet 5: 8). God has given him the power to burden us, to attack us through our evil passions. He is filled with envy and hatred toward us. He attacks God in us. This is an enemy against whom we are quite unevenly matched so far as our natural human defenses go.

The world is in league with the devil. By this we mean those who live for the satisfaction of their own pride, sensuality, and self-love. They are not content to do wrong in their own persons. They approve of sin fundamentally and look upon it as a right—as one of the benefits of mankind. They live for money and the indulgence of the senses. In their opinion voluntary poverty and chastity amount to madness. They think that anyone who accepts humiliation and insult must be mentally disturbed. Prayers are for those who have nothing better to do. They try to convert us to their way of thinking. They would like to entice us on to the broad road that leads to destruction. They try to tire us out by holding our thoughts and our lives, our religion and our Church up to ridicule and insult.

Temptation does not always come from people who are downright pagans. Many who are simply not practical Christians lead us astray by their example and advice. They do most harm by turning us, through flattery, vanity, and sensuality, against our better judgment. Greed and passion from within—the world and the devil from without—truly there is no lack of enticements and snares to draw us away from good into the vortex of sin.

Meanwhile, what is God's attitude? "Let no man, when he is tempted, say that he is tempted by God" (James 1: 13). How could God be holy if He tempted us to evil? He does not tempt us. He merely permits temptation to assail us from within and without. He is master of the tempter, who can only try us as much as the Lord allows. He "will not suffer you to be tempted above that ye are able but will with the temptation also make a way to escape, that ye may be able to bear it."

By permitting us, in His divine wisdom, to be tempted, God has a providential purpose. If He did not know how to turn temptations to our good, He would not permit them. Temptations are not a disaster but a blessing. Why? Because they are an indispensable help in the task of cleansing the heart. Like lightning they penetrate the darkest recesses, revealing the greed, the self-love, sensuality, and selfishness, pride, avarice, and unloving qualities that lurk in our heart. Hence they become aids to self-knowledge and humility. In temptation we discover unmistakably how weak we are when left to our own resources and how little is needed to divert us from the right path. They spur us on to be brave in resisting them. Thus we are led to repent our former neglect and laziness. They compel us to be vigilant and to avoid everything that might lead to temptation. They force us to wrestle zealously in prayer. For, if we are to stand firm, we need the help of grace, and grace comes through prayer.

Temptation is a valuable means of speeding the soul's progress. For this reason it is a very good thing. No one who honestly strives for perfection in God can bypass temptation. It keeps us from falling into a state of drowsiness and neglect. It drives us to contrition and sacrifice. Especially has it the function and the power to increase us in virtue. Every temptation we fight and conquer is a victory for virtue and augments the strength of virtue. We are called upon to combat unbelief and thereby strengthen our faith. We defend ourselves against the intrusion of suspicion of hatred, of envy, of unloving thoughts, and in so doing perform an act of love. We despise a sensation of pride that rises in us, and so add to our humility.

Where would our virtue be if we had no temptations to combat? In the struggle against temptation our virtue becomes purer, stronger, more constant. In conquering a distaste for prayer and religious exercises, we grow in loyalty to God. If we are abused and persecuted, we learn to rise above lawlessness and the fear of men, attaining amid inner freedom that light in which we perceive only God and God's will. Can we therefore say that temptation is not a blessing?

Temptation is a first-class incentive to good deeds by which we may earn eternal life. Every temptation we overcome increases sanctifying grace in us, and we open our souls to a more abundant inflow of the divine life that links us to God in Christ, the body. "Knowing this, that the trying of your faith worketh patience. But let patience have her perfect work that ye may be perfect and entire, wanting nothing" (James 1: 3–4). This is the fruit of temptations effectively repelled.

How can we wonder or complain that so many temptations have to be met? "Because God greatly loved thee, he let temptation light upon thee." With these words the angel comforted Tobias. Temptations are the reward of earnest zeal, of faithfulness to God. God permits them to befall us, so that we may become purer and more pleasing to Him. Should we therefore desire to be spared temptation? Hardly, when we realize that, properly viewed, temptations are a great aid to progress, to the fulfillment of a life of grace, growth in consciousness of kinship with God in Christ, the body, whose members we are.

2. HOW WE CAN FIGHT TEMPTATION

It would be the height of recklessness to wish for temptation or to do anything that would draw it upon us without cause.

On the other hand, it is wrong to be frightened of temptation—as though God did not give us the necessary grace to withstand it. We ought not to allow temptation to depress us, nor to believe that all is lost. After all, we do not stand alone. God is loyal. He does not "suffer you to be tempted beyond that ye are able." God proves His loyalty, not by shielding us against all temptation: that would do us more harm than good; but by not permitting us to be tried beyond our strength. In any case, do we not owe this strength to Him, to His grace? He keeps temptation in check and prevents it from becoming too great for us to cope with. He gives us greater temptations for greater grace, so that we may be steadfast and conquer. He loves us and knows what is going on in our hearts. He has the greatest possible interest in our struggle and our victory.

Yes, He lives in us, the Father, the Son, and the Holy Spirit, "closer than breathing," supporting us, and helping us to conquer. He lives in Christ, the body, the vine. His strength flows through us. He is entirely on our side in the fight against the world, the flesh, and the devil. "I have overcome the world" (Jn 16: 33). We can depend upon His strength, which is active in us. "I can do all things in Him who strengtheneth me" (Phil 4: 13). What should we fear, since we have received the seal of the cross in Baptism and are illuminated by the light of Christ? Since we have been taken up into His life, that we may live it with Him? "For he hath given his angels charge over thee, to keep thee in all ways" (Ps 90: 11).

So, with God and Christ, the Savior, we can courageously meet the challenge of temptation:

(a) We do so with a clear perception that recognizes in temptation three distinct stages—the first incitement, followed by attraction of the lower instincts and final acquiescence of our higher nature. The enemy, or our imagination, offers us the forbidden fruit, sometimes in a very urgent way, with great insistence and obstinacy. But this is the very first stage, the incitement, the preliminary whisper. In no way does it amount to sin as long as we reject it. Temptation goes further. Unconsciously, our lower instincts are attracted by the forbidden fruit so seductively offered. They find a certain pleasure in it. This necessarily reacts upon our will and inclines it to cooperate. Now is the decisive moment. If the will rejects the presumption energetically, the battle is won. But the soul may waver in indecision. Its judgment may be insufficiently balanced, or it may reject the proffered fruit only when it feels that acceptance may be dangerous.

There is another state, in which reason is not quite clear. The will is caught to a certain extent in the lust of the lower instincts. It is a state of involuntary yielding; and in that state it cannot be a question of a conscious sin. But it is a different matter when with full deliberation and consent we yield to the temptation—that is, when, in spite of the promptings of conscience, we accept the forbidden fruit and partake of it with enjoyment. In its most important form this complete and voluntary surrender to temptation is a mortal sin, in its less important form a venial sin; but both are deliberate and fully conscious sins.

(b) We overcome temptation by earnest and unrelenting attrition of the inner man. Attrition must be linked with prayer. "Watch and pray, that ye enter not into temptation." The devil's tactics, and the world's, are to keep us from praying. They try to instill in us a repugnance to prayer. We do well to avoid all opportunities that might lead even to the smallest sin or failing. "He who loves danger succumbs to it." It is one thing to plunge into danger in fulfillment of a duty but quite another to court temptation to sin without any valid reason. How many have done their souls almost irreparable harm by rushing into unnecessary risk just for the sake of some superfluous experience. We can also circumvent temptation by hard work—by the zealous performance of our duties or by ministering to others. "The devil finds work for idle hands to do," says the old proverb.

We can also protect ourselves against temptation by developing a genuine horror of sin, even of the smallest and apparently most insignificant failings. But above all we must apply ourselves earnestly to the task of cultivating our love of God and the divine Savior. Love is the greatest help, the most powerful shield against temptation. Loves gives us strength and the impulse to be happy, both of which are powerful in overcoming temptation. We draw the power to love from participation in Mass and in Holy Communion, the sacrament of love.

(c) In the battle against temptation we pray constantly and with complete confidence: "Lead us not into temptation"— that is, give us strength to resist temptation. Since our divine Savior Himself taught us to pray, "Lead us not into temptation," we surely do well to repeat that petition over and over. In doing so, we lean upon Him who destroyed the power of Satan by His passion and death (Jn 12: 31). We also combat temptation by going often to confession. Half the battle is won when we acquaint our confessor with the temptations assailing us, confident in the knowledge that God gives the priest grace to offer the right counsel and guidance. This revealing of temptations was a sacred matter to our fathers, who adhered to it with great strictness. They knew why— for the act of humility is a most effective means of overcoming the tempter and putting him to flight.

We battle against temptation but not in such a way as to let ourselves in for an argument. Nor should we fight temptation directly: the best methods are indirect. As soon as temptation raises its head, we look the other way, directing our attention to our Savior and clinging to Him . . . with an act of humble submission, an act of confidence in Him and His closeness to us, an act of petition for His help and His strength. In this way temptation is marvelously transformed into an aid to prayer, opening the way to a closer union with

God and our Savior, Jesus Christ, our Lord. "To them that love God, all things work together unto good" (Rom 8: 28).

★   ★   ★

TEMPTATION, properly speaking, is a grace, a mighty help in the building up of a life of Christian virtue. That is what God intends it to be; that is how we must look upon it.

As baptized Christians, we know ourselves to be members of Christ. In this secure consciousness we can counter temptation with Christ's strength. We are able to conquer. "I can do all things in him that strengtheneth me."

"Blessed is he that endureth temptation, for when he hath been proved, he shall receive the crown of life" (1 James 1: 12).

10. *First Thoughts and Emotions*

> *To them that love God, all things work together unto good.*
>
> ROMANS 8: 28

THERE IS one special form of temptation that raises its head in the first thoughts and emotions we are constantly experiencing. First impressions—the moment we become aware of anything—produce a natural, involuntary reaction that determines our later attitude. Sometimes it calls forth judgments that are unloving or rebellious—thoughts based on self-sufficiency or vanity, on envy, jealousy, superiority, bitterness, anger, impatience or curiosity, sensuality, attraction, and repulsion; a whole wilderness of involuntary thoughts and emotions that take priority over free will and cause us, generally speaking, a great deal of trouble.

1. WHAT THEY ARE AND WHAT THEY MEAN

(a) First thoughts and emotions are not sins. They are natural and necessary processes, leading to the determination of free will. It is inevitable that a nature not yet perfect should have, for example, impulses of envy and jealousy the moment it sees more honor paid to a fellow man. It depends largely on the nature of an individual—whether he is drawn to certain people, repelled by others. Some people are by nature quickly excited when anything goes wrong—when their will is crossed or their plans or wishes miscarry. A man may do his utmost to rise above physical desires to a more spiritual plane and yet continue to have the most disturbingly sensual thoughts and desires.

First thoughts and emotions, carrying within them the germs of temptation, are a true cross to be borne by the aspirant to virtue; they are trials sent by God in His divine love. God allows us to be subject to these reactions in order that they may reduce us to shame and show us our own inner corruption; how much in us is still ugly, lawless, unworthy, perverted, and ignoble; how mean and unspiritual we are in our thoughts, judgments, wishes, impulses, feelings, attractions, and repulsions.

(b) The cross is a healing medium. That is God's purpose in the many painful and humiliating thoughts and emotions He allows us to experience. If we approach these perversions in the right way, we can draw healing benefits from our pride and self-conceit, from our self-satisfaction and self-love. This healing comes about when we recognize how wicked and selfish, how small-minded, mean, and ill-intentioned we are by nature, and how greatly we stand in need of God's help and grace. They can actually become a means of healing. Daily and hourly these thoughts and emotions give us renewed proof of our inner corruption. As we recognize what our faults are, we become willing to learn, and this fortifies us in the virtue that is the foundation and necessary starting point of all virtue—humility. "It is good for me that thou hast humbled me; that I may learn justification" (Ps 118: 71).

These thoughts and feelings can become indispensable aids to virtue and holiness. An emotion contrary to love may arise. No sooner are we aware of this than our will steps in to counteract the thought—and a blow has been struck for the virtue of love. We may become aware of a prompting to impatience. At once we turn to our Lord, declaring ourselves ready to submit to the unpleasantness with which we are faced—and thereby practice the virtue of patience. A feeling of self-satisfaction may arise in us. It reminds us that we are still in bondage to personal pride. Instantly we convert the thought into an act of humility. We meet the first stirrings of sensuality with the assertion "I belong to Thee, O Lord," and a prayer for the virtue of chastity stands to our account. In this manner, first thoughts and emotions become daily and hourly opportunities to strengthen ourselves in virtue, in grace. In fact, we should be deprived of endless opportunities if God sent us no first thoughts and emotions. All that is necessary is to recognize these impromptu inner processes and to handle them in the right way.

2. HOW WE MUST HANDLE THEM

Not only our peace of mind but also the development of our inner life in its striving toward virtue hinges largely on the manner in which we relate ourselves for practical purposes to first thoughts and emotions. Here we come to the parting of ways. Should we take the left-hand road, which leads to self-indulgence and self-love, or the right-hand road of self-humiliation and loving submission to the cross that is laid upon us?

(a) Many allow themselves to be confused by first thoughts and emotions. They regard them as sins that cannot be overcome and, discouraged, give up the struggle before it has really begun. Others believe they can eventually rid themselves of these thoughts and emotions and imagine that perfection will have been reached if only they can accomplish this task. They are unhappy and angry that such feelings keep recurring; so beset with self-love and secret pride they are. Many, if not most of us, are not quite clear in their minds about these thoughts and emotions and adopt a defensive attitude toward them. Consequently, such people become excited and nervous. They live in daily apprehension lest a feeling of self-satisfaction, an impure idea, an unloving thought, or a momentary impulse of impatience should assail them. Without knowing it, they increase their tendency to these reactions by their very effort to repress them. Sinking deeper and deeper into remorse and confusion, they subject themselves to mental torture and become victims to the very self-preoccupations with which they are trying to fight their rebellious feelings.

(b) Certainly we are obliged to fight our rebellious feelings, but in the right way. The most important point is to see them in true perspective—that is, as things that God sends to spur us on to perfection in virtue. We do not desire them—and we must never lose sight of this. But we must submit humbly and patiently to the recognition of our failings and acknowledge our unworthiness.

Instead of this, we so often go to work at them the wrong way by asserting ourselves and seeking forcefully to repress them. We take pains to knock on the head everything that awakens in us. It is almost as if our piety demanded to be shielded against all annoyances; as if we had no right to experience waves of impatience, displeasure, sensuality; as if we were in some way superior to such weaknesses. That is why we are excited when we become aware of these stirrings and seek every means to protect ourselves against them. But the more earnestly we fight against them the more obstinately they remain entrenched, plaguing us with their persistence. That is where we make our mistake. We see in them only troublemakers, temptations, and that brings us to a halt. Instead, we should see God behind these things and turn to Him at once, taking the cross from His hands. "It is Thy will that I should bear this cross? Thy will be done."

The correct course is not to be on the defensive against these thoughts and emotions, seeking to exterminate them by force, but to accept them and turn them to our own use. We can use them for strengthening virtue, in a spirit of humble self-examination. How ugly I still am in my thoughts and judgments, full of selfishness and sensuality! We acknowledge the fact that we are still corrupt and perverted, bowing quietly and patiently under the cross of spiritual poverty. From this act of humility we proceed to an act of trust in Him who is so near with His grace and help. This is how the first thought, the first emotion, the temptation, becomes a means to humility to prayer—an act of virtue. Virtue is awakened, strengthened, confirmed, and fulfilled through these first thoughts and emotions.

We can go a step farther and daily renew our resolution never to give way to these first feelings. It all depends upon the fundamental attitude of our will. If we give our will-power a strong, firm, clear direction, it daily becomes better able and more resolved to avoid the wrong path as soon as we recognize it, more resolved to seize upon any aid that would keep it at peak level, more positive in striving for virtue, more resolute in attrition and in embracing the sacrifices and efforts that a pure, God-informed love demands. Such a will avoids anxiety and nervous unrest when mad thoughts and various emotions agitate it. It does not allow itself to be drawn into combat with them or waste its strength fighting every single stir of thought. It lets the hounds bark and, without taking any further notice of them, passes them by. "Smash rebellion, perverted thoughts, on Christ as soon as they rise," advises the Holy Father St. Benedict in chapter 4 of his Rule—a valuable precept. Instead of paying heed to these thoughts and suggestions, halting, granting them admission, and occupying ourselves with them, we turn, almost without noticing them, to the opposite side, to Christ. "I belong to Thee. Do Thou help me."

Thus the thoughts and emotions that sought to plague us actually lead us to the Savior, directing our eyes to Him, prompting us to renew our surrender, our loyalty, our love to Him. A golden rule, simple and reliable: instead of torturing ourselves with errant thoughts and sensual emotions, we learn the divine art of turning them to our advantage. Then they not only teach us self-knowledge and humility; they impel us again and again toward God, toward the Savior, bringing Him our trust and asking His help. They also make us vigilant in attrition and faithful in little things. Thus, far from being a hindrance to our progress, they can become a reliable road to virtue.

God is love. "All things work together for good to them

that love God." Even the many burdensome first thoughts and emotions can lead us to salvation, to the fulfillment of grace and virtue, if we use them properly and learn how to make the most of them.

This must be our motto: Take them and use them; do not reject them.

11. *Imperfections*

Follow after love.
I CORINTHIANS 14: 1

To LIVE the life of Jesus Christ, completely sharing with Him the life of His divine body, the vine. . . . But in Him there is no sin, not even the smallest imperfection. Whatever He does, He does perfectly; outwardly in effect, as well as inwardly, as befits His blameless intention. It is impossible for Him to do anything from a starting point of less than perfect love: the fear motive or the hope of reward never enters into any of His actions. He does everything out of pure love for the Father, entirely for God's will, for His honor and delight. He lives the life of perfect prayer, perfect truth, perfect fulfillment, perfect praise and thanksgiving, petition and intercession. His attrition is perfect in every aspect. His readiness for sacrifice recognizes no limits other than the delight of the Father.

His love of purity, His renunciation, and His humility before man are heroic; equally so is His love of mankind. His heart is free from bitterness even toward His deadly enemies. He is forever offering Himself up to renewed injustice, meekly following His persecutors to more torture. He gives His life and His blood for friends and enemies alike. Not one single thing remains that He could have done better. All that He prays, speaks, does, or suffers and the manner in which He prays, speaks, works, and suffers are so good and perfect that they cannot be bettered. They are all works and actions that give the Father endless delight and that redound to His eternal honor.

To relive this life in us, with Him, is our high calling. That means not only the elimination of all sin but also a ceaseless battle for freedom from imperfections, which tend to cling even to our good deeds, thoughts, and intentions.

I. THE FACT: WE DO MUCH GOOD IMPERFECTLY

(a) "It becometh us to fulfill all justice" (Mt 3: 15)—that is to say, to do everything that we do perfectly. God does not forbid us all human affection, but he commands that our love should be first for His honor and glory. He does not command us to sell all our property and give the proceeds to the poor in order to follow Him, but He recommends it. "If thou wilt be perfect, go and sell what thou hast, and give to the poor, and come and follow me." He recommends us to serve with humility. "He that is the greatest among you shall be your servant" (Mt 23: 11). "When thou are invited, go, sit down in the lowest place" (Lk 14: 10). "Be not solicitous, saying: What shall we eat? Or what shall we drink? Or wherewith shall we be clothed? For after all these things do the heathen seek. For your Father knoweth that you have need of all these things. Seek ye first the kingdom of God and his justice [i.e., what is right before God], and all these things shall be added unto you" (Mt 7: 12). "I say to you not to resist evil; but if one strike thee on thy right cheek, turn to him also the other. And if any man will contend with thee in judgment [unjustly], and take away thy coat, let go thy cloak also unto him. And whosoever will force thee one mile, go with him two others. Give to him that asketh of thee, and from him that would borrow of thee turn not away" (Mt 5: 39–42). He does not command it; He advises it.

If we do anything that is commanded, we fulfill the law. So far as the commandments are concerned we have no sin upon our conscience. But beyond all this, beyond that which cannot be done or left undone without sin, the whole world is open with possibilities for our endeavor in pursuit of perfection, by following the Lord's recommendations and suggestions. We are advised not only to do what is right and good but what is better—what is no longer law but a matter of perfection. At this peak there can be no lukewarmness, no more venial sin or failings. Ceaseless striving, burning zeal rules here; no opportunity of doing good must be missed, no inner prompting to good ignored.

All this must happen in an attitude of complete self-abandon and conform to the highest standard of perfection we can attain. We must never resist an urge to do good or leave undone any good we can possibly do; we must never miss an opportunity of doing good or of going from good to better. That is what we mean by "loving zealously." The love that loves God above all things, loves Him so deeply, so strongly, so genuinely and completely that it rules out anything less than perfection, anything that might displease Him. In this love we live completely for His honor, glory, and delight.

When we come to the limits of strict duty as laid down by the commandments, a wide field of possible imperfection stretches before us. We fail, for instance, even when we obey the strict letter of the law, by ignoring whatever may lie beyond the minimum essentials, leaving the "perfect works" to those more perfect than ourselves. With many people this attitude is habitual, one might almost say fundamental. We also fail if we perform our good deeds negligently, letting them fall short of the standard that should be our target if we aim at perfection. We could all improve in our prayers, our studies, our work, and in the love we bear toward one another. None of us does as much good as we are able.

(b) We burden our souls daily with many imperfections. We are in a state of sanctifying grace. Therefore, everything we do is either a sin or a thing pleasing to God and worthy of reward. There is practically nothing between these two extremes. Comparatively speaking, opportunities to fall into venial sin are less numerous than chances of doing good. The schedule for a good day might consist of prayer, work, service of love, attrition, suffering. Yet imperfection tacks itself onto this practically unbroken succession of meritorious acts. We may perform good deeds negligently, with not so much devotion, or from such blameless motives that they could not be improved upon. They could be performed even more carefully, more unselfishly, with greater love of God.

Our supernatural good works, such as prayer, obedience, attrition, overcoming, love of our neighbors and enemies, and religious practices of all kinds, are often prompted by imperfect motives. They do not always spring from pure love of God; more often such factors as fear, hope of reward or success or blessing enter into them. We seek God, but for our own sake, because we seek our "luck" in Him or at any rate some good that we desire. Lacking the perfect motive, pure love of God, many, very many, of our good deeds fall short of perfection.

Moreover, many of our good deeds are performed with very little love, certainly not the love that springs from zealous hearts. This again is the source of numerous imperfections.

Our natural, or secular, good deeds, such as work, fulfillment of duty in the home and in our profession, in eating and drinking, rest, recreation, care of our bodies, our studies, and so on, which in themselves are pleasing to God, often become imperfect because they are not performed in a spirit of faith or not influenced by supernatural considerations. They spring from our natural human way of seeing, considering, and judging things. Hence, it results in a large number of imperfect acts and deeds.

We often have good impulses—for instance, an impulse to pray. Yet we prefer to do something else that may in itself be quite harmless, some task that could be easily postponed. Although we are fully aware that it would be better (i.e., more pleasing to God) if we obeyed the impulse, we ignore it and go our own way. Another good action rendered imperfect.

A terrifying source of imperfection is our inborn habit of

concentrating, when we do good, not on God, but on ourselves. We judge everything—events, experiences and incidents, conditions, people—from our own standpoint. We pronounce a thing good only insofar as it pleases us. We call a thing bad because it is not as we would like it to be. Whether it is pleasing or not pleasing to God does not trouble us in the least. It is almost as though we had forgotten Him altogether, such precedence we give to ourselves. We consider our prayers and our reception of the sacraments good when it falls out that they bring us personal satisfaction. Always "I" in the first place, God a long way behind . . . results in countless imperfect acts and deeds throughout the day.

St. John of the Cross develops in his book *The Dark Night of the Senses* a revealing picture of imperfection among pious and zealous souls (see book II, chap. 2). We detract from the good we do with so many shortcomings, and we attach so little importance to them. This greatly retards our inner progress. "As long as these shortcomings are there, it is lost labor to strive for perfection" (St. John of the Cross).

How is it that we underrate imperfections so much—even when we resolve to avoid all venial sin and actually succeed in doing so? It is because we persuade ourselves that it is enough to refrain from sin and because we are seldom seriously convinced that we are really called to a life of perfection, a spiritual life in which imperfection of any kind simply has no place.

2. THE EFFECT OF IMPERFECTIONS

(a) An imperfect act is in itself a good act, not a sin, not a trespass against any commandment or prohibition of God. But it could and should be a better act than it is. We easily set our conscience at rest by saying: "I am not bound to do more. I have done what duty demands, and I always do my duty." But we forget that an imperfectly performed action can easily become a venial sin. In certain circumstances it may already be a sin, according to the motive that caused us to act imperfectly. It might be an excessive attachment to some form of work, to some person, or to a mild pleasure that in itself is quite harmless. It might be a defect of character, such as love of personal comfort or convenience, unwillingness to make sacrifices, lack of faith in relating supernatural considerations to practical everyday life. It might even be want of self-control or an attitude of easygoing superficiality in relation to the divine. Deep down, we may trace all imperfections to self-love, selfishness, and insufficient control of our personal pride. Any of these causes, which render so many good deeds imperfect, may easily turn the imperfections into sins. Hence they may become subjects for the confessional, although, we repeat, imperfections are not actually sins, apart from the motives that lie behind them.

(b) Imperfection is in itself no sin, but it is an irregularity. At best, it can be described as the very opposite of what God, the Savior, expects of us. We show ourselves positively disrespectful to God when we offer up imperfections. They signify that we are prepared to serve Him only for the sake of avoiding sin and thus escaping punishment. Properly considered, imperfection means nothing less than the repulsion of God's will, setting our own pleasure above it. We seek primarily what pleases ourselves, though we take the precaution of not actually breaking God's commandments, and for self-satisfaction choose acts not directly offensive to God. We are inclined to view activities that are good in themselves, such as work, duty, and so on, not as a means of pleasing God, joyously performing them because they are His will for us, but from our own personal standpoint, as to whether they are pleasant, useful, or profitable to us. We are often so much occupied with these considerations that we do not think of God at all. Ourselves first; then God and His wishes: Is that perfect love of God?

Imperfection lessens the good we should do and are able to do. It diminishes the moral effect of any good we do and decidedly retards our growth in grace, in eternal glory. It is self-evident that we forfeit many divine blessings in this way. We can never attain to full perfection, to complete integration in the life of God, while we harbor imperfections in our soul.

Imperfections rob our soul of true nobility and the urge to soar. If not constantly checked, they cling to all our actions, lowering our whole capacity to such an extent that it cannot unfold. Yes, our imperfections can easily lead to backsliding in spiritual life. Undesirable tendencies inevitably creep in where disregarded imperfections become habitual, and these smooth the path of venial sin.

Love is weakened by the many impediments that choke it, and then the trouble begins. We should continually grow in love, but imperfections prevent this. It becomes impossible to fulfill the commandment "Thou shalt love the Lord thy God." Then we cease to make progress. Our soul's growth stops. When a child's growth is arrested, it becomes a dwarf, a freak. Exactly the same thing happens to our inner life. No longer fed by love, it shrivels, goes into a decline. How many of these little abnormalities there are—poor, dwarfed souls! Simply for want of dealing firmly with our imperfections, some become careless, indifferent—and then . . . !

Imperfect good deeds are not to be dismissed lightly. We cannot get away from them with the comforting thought that, after all, we have not fallen into venial sin. We still have a long way to go! Whoever fails to go forward, seeking day by day to work harder, pray more seriously, increase in faith, love, humility, and patience, is bound to slip back. Either we grow better, more perfect, or we deteriorate. We cannot stand still; there is no such thing. We must keep moving, either one way or the other. Let us take this to heart. Just as the attitude we adopt toward venial sin is all-important, the same applies to imperfections. Our inner progress in grace and virtue, and our greater or lesser reward in eternity, depend upon that attitude.

★   ★   ★

THE PROPHET Elijah came to Beersheba and went a day's journey into the wilderness of Judea. He lay down under a juniper tree to die. "It is enough for me, O Lord; take away my soul." He slept. Then "an angel touched him and said to him: Arise and eat. He looked, and behold, there was at his head a hearth, a cake, and a vessel of water. And he ate and drank, and he fell asleep again. And the angel of the Lord came again the second time, and touched him, and said, Arise, eat: for thou hast yet a great way to go. And he arose, and ate and drank, and walked in the strength of that food forty days and forty nights unto the mount of God, Horeb" (1 Kings 19: 3–8).

In the prophet Elijah we may recognize ourselves. We should often like to say: "It is enough." Is it really enough that we should try so hard to keep our soul unstained by sin? Every intentional sin? Is it not enough that we should subject ourselves to constant attrition, so that we may not fall even into semivoluntary venial sin through haste, surprise, or momentary weakness? It might appear to be enough. But the angel of God, divine grace, wakes us out of our meditation and says: "Arise, you have a long way to go"—till you have overcome all imperfection as far as is possible here on earth.

How can this be? There is only one way—the perfect way, through pure love of God and Christ. Everything centers upon the growth of our love (1 Cor 14: 1). We should ask ourselves: What has been my attitude toward imperfections up to now? What have I thought about them? Have I taken them seriously?

We must pray for grace to reach the point where, with the zeal of love, we do all the good we are prompted to do, or have opportunity to do, and do it perfectly.

12. *Humility*

PART I

Learn of me, because I am meek, and humble of heart.
MATTHEW 11: 29

BECAUSE we are *in Christ*, limbs of His body, the vine, we are called to live the Christ-life . . . to live His life with Him. The life of the body flows into the limbs. The strength and life of the vine are revealed by the branches. If our life is to be that of a limb or branch of Christ, it must embody a spirit of humility. It is precisely of humility that our Lord speaks when He says, "Learn of me." It is as though He would convince us that everything depends upon learning the art of being humble. We should think of ourselves humbly, recognize that we are as insignificant as the dust from which we sprang. . . . Cheerfully considering ourselves of no account and choosing the road of Christian humility in our whole thought and intention, our labors and our sufferings. The spirit of Christ is essentially a spirit of humility. Therefore the spirit that flows through the limbs, the branches of Christ, must also be a spirit of humility. "Learn of me; I am humble of heart."

I. WHAT CHRISTIAN HUMILITY IS

(a) Our Lord Himself gives us the best definition of humility. "Two men went up into the temple to pray; the one a Pharisee, and the other a publican. The Pharisee, standing, prayed thus with himself: God, I give thee thanks, that I am not as the rest of men, extortioners, unjust, adulterers, as also is this publican. I fast twice in a week; I give tithes of all that I possess. And the publican, standing afar off, would not so much as lift up his eyes toward Heaven; but struck his breast, saying: O God, be merciful to me a sinner. I say to you, this man went down into his house justified rather than the other; because everyone that exalteth himself shall be humbled, and he that humbleth himself shall be exalted" (Lk 18: 10–14).

(b) Pride is the inordinate value we place on our own merit. The proud man gives himself credit for all that is good in him, as though he had given virtue to himself. Pride makes a man well pleased with himself. He likes to think of his talents, his wisdom, his gains through his own cleverness, his brilliant achievements. He likes other people to notice them, too—he likes others to think well of him, to praise him, talk about him, marvel at him. This is self-satisfaction, and self-satisfaction leads to self-confidence. The proud man relies on his own capabilities, his own understanding and insight; he doesn't need the advice and help of others. He considers himself more competent, cleverer than other people; so he has no need to pray for light, strength, and guidance. He is sufficient unto himself.

Self-satisfaction implies superiority. The proud man despises others, looks down on them, considers himself their better—in short, behaves exactly like the Pharisee in the parable.

Self-satisfaction also leads to misplaced ambition—that is, to an inordinate desire for glory, admiration, recognition, a celebrated name; and with all this goes a fear of not being sufficiently respected, sufficiently appreciated—a fear of being forgotten, overlooked, ignored. Jealousy, too, lest someone else should compete with him and achieve higher honor, more success, more recognition and influence.

Thus the evils of envy, contempt, and hate grow out of

pride and sometimes even the bitterest enmity. The ambitious man desires to have priority everywhere. He wants to domineer, always to be considered in the right. He may even become ludicrous, always trying to enforce his own opinion, his own will. He covers up his weakness, his failings, as much as he can, and takes refuge in bluff, so that after a time he becomes dishonest, two-faced, undependable—a tortured slave to flattery and the fear of other people's opinions.

The humble man looks first to God. "Thou alone art great." The humble man knows that of himself he is nothing and possesses nothing. Of course he sees the good that he has, just as the proud man sees his; but he is under no misapprehension about it. "What hast thou that thou hast not received?" (1 Cor 4: 7). He humbles himself in acknowledging his unworthiness and complete dependence on God and never steps out of the position to which he properly belongs in relation to his Maker.

Humility is a quality of spiritual insight. A humble person clearly recognizes that of himself he is nothing, has nothing; nothing under nature—neither life, nor a body, nor spirit, nor talents, nor strength, nor health, nor hands, nor eyes—nothing, absolutely nothing; nothing under grace. "God it is who works in us to will and to be perfect," says St. Paul. "Not that we are sufficient to think anything of ourselves, as of ourselves; but our sufficiency is from God" (2 Cor 3: 5). There is not one single thought, no healthy or good decision, not one good work, no matter how insignificant, no prayer, no act of faith or of love that we can call exclusively our own. Even as far as we work through divine grace, which God has bestowed on us, and do not misuse it, the fruit of grace is the work of God in us. "What would you have, had you not received?" asks the Apostle. Nothing, absolutely nothing.

Then, sin and sinfulness. . . . The humble person recognizes that there is only one thing he can do of himself: commit sin. He knows that in consequence of human nature he is capable of every sin. If he has not fallen into this, that, or the other sin, it is not because of his own merit, but because only of the love of God, which has shielded him from sin. With the publican he acknowledges himself a sinner, unworthy to lift his eyes to God, unworthy to be respected, admired, honored, or loved by his fellow man. Worthy only to be recognized and rated for what he is, a sinner.

Humility is best expressed by a humble way of regulating our actions. He who is truly humble does not think of high regard, of making himself important either in his own person or through the enforcement of his will, his wishes, and his plans. He wants, in fact, he requests, to suffer, to be disregarded, treated with indignity; he suffers contempt and injustice with the same humility that our obedient, rejected Savior showed toward His persecutors. He counts it as the greatest joy to stand beside our Lord, as a limb of His body, obediently allowing himself to be pushed into the background and forgotten, to be ill-treated and loaded with injustice. He lives the humble life of our Lord and reckons it an honor to do so. Filled with the spirit of Christ, he does not try to escape from lowly, humiliating conditions; he does not strive to rise, to shine in splendid achievements, high offices, honors. He is content in his moderate powers and talents, in the work entrusted to him. Quite content, too, that others should do better for themselves than he does.

The humble person is especially conscious of his faults and failings. He recognizes his inconstancy, the little acts of neglect into which he daily falls. He freely admits his faults and deficiencies, pleading guilty to more defects and deficiencies than others have. He is so convinced of his nothingness and unworthiness that he considers himself the least among men, the greatest sinner, and is too ashamed to lift his eyes to Heaven.

The more he becomes aware of his helplessness, the more he leans upon God and the Savior's mercy, grace, forgiveness, help, presence. No one prays more earnestly than the truly humble man. No one wrestles more sincerely for light and strength than he. No one has more unshakable trust in God's help—and God in return gives him grace: to none is it more bounteously given than to the truly humble. God loves to create from nothing. In God, in his Savior, the humble man is strong, eager, fearless, enterprising; not afraid to undertake any task, shoulder any burden—equal to any suffering or renunciation. "I can do all things in Him who strengthens me."

The humble man grasps the inner meaning of the words "The very hairs of your head are numbered" (Mt 10: 30). He recognizes in this statement that there is nothing outside God's will. He sees in everything the glory of Providence and divine order. He throws himself trustfully into the arms of this living Providence. His whole life is a joyous surrender to the will and pleasure of God. Even when he is in the depths of misery he is undisturbed, for he sees not his own distressing condition but God's mercy, forgiveness, and love. He is happy even while conscious of his own imperfections. He does not desire imperfections: he despises his failings and fights against them, but they do not disturb him—they only make him more humble and drive him more often to God in prayer and trust. He would like to hasten with all his might to the heights of divine life and love, but he is content, even though his progress is slow and laborious, recognizing the many demerits detaining him. He takes everything as it comes in complete surrender to the guidance and providence of God. All he wants is to be quite small and insignificant, quite poor in spirit, yielding himself into the arms of God. Who is more inwardly free, more completely liberated from guilt and worry, more content or nearer to God than he who is truly humble?

That is the mystery of humility—to be nothing in one's own eyes or the eyes of others, to be despised for the will of God and the Savior. How little we Christians understand this mystery and its secret bliss! The cup is bitter, very bitter, but it is only the cup; and what it contains is unspeakably sweet.

2. WHY HUMILITY?

The Church needs humble souls. "Suffer little children to come unto me, for theirs is the kingdom of Heaven" (Mt 19: 14)—of grace, virtue, and holiness. Truly humble souls are rare. They are vastly outnumbered by others we meet, hypocritical souls, full of self-satisfaction, seeking praise and recognition, honor, respect; pompous souls puffed up with self-importance, eloquent about their own achievements, good works, efforts, sufferings, grace, and progress; souls bursting with conceit, caprice, and self-will, having no esteem whatever for others. So many pious ones, without knowing it, are the very Pharisees of the Gospel, praying in the secrecy of their hearts: "Lord, I thank Thee that I am not as others are."

(a) As pride is the spirit of the world, so humility is the virtue of Christ. "The Word was made flesh and dwelt amongst us" (Jn 1: 14). The mystery of God made man is the mystery of God's eternal condescension and self-expression in Christ, His Son. God's positive hunger for humiliation, degradation, ignominy, is incomprehensible to our human understanding. "Who, being in the form of God, . . . emptied himself, taking the form of a servant, being made in the likeness of men. . . . He humbled himself, becoming obedient unto death, even to the death of the cross" (Phil 2: 6–8). The Son of God, eternal, divine Wisdom, freely chose the degradation and ignominy of crucifixion. *Learn of me. . . . Live my life with me. . . .*

We follow our Lord to the stable at Bethlehem, into the retired life of poverty, of labor and obedience at Nazareth. God's Son voluntarily, and with fully conscious decision, chooses lowliness. He could have had a different life, but he deliberately chose a humble place. *Learn of me. . . . Live my life with me.*

We follow Him to the Mount of Olives, to the eve of that tragic Good Friday. There He stands in the soiled robe of sin. "Him, who knew no sin, he hath made sin for us; that we might be made the justice of God in him" (2 Cor 5: 21). How soiled, how humbly He stands before the pure eyes of the Father! Could He have taken upon Himself greater ignominy than the sins of the whole of humanity—the sins of pride, sensuality, of injustice and uncharitableness, of lewdness, starting with the sin of Eve and Adam, the sin of Cain right down to the very last sin that will be committed before the Day of Judgment? We can understand why, on the Mount of Olives, blood gushed from His pores in the agony of comprehension. It was the flood of shame that rose in Him at the sins with which He knew Himself to be weighed down. All this He took upon Himself quite voluntarily, out of pure love. *Learn of me. Live my life with me. . . .*

How He humbled Himself as he stood beside the prisoner Barabbas, with the people who had so recently hailed Him with "Hosannah, Son of David!" now calling to Pilate: "Give us Barabbas free!" What of Him, the guiltless one? He bears it all silently, this ignominy heaped upon Him in full view of the heathen Roman Empire, as represented by Pilate, and in the face of the whole Jewish populace. He bears it without a word of reproach—not one word against the injustice of authority, of His own people, condemning Him who has done no wrong to the shameful death of the lowest of lawbreakers. There He stands, hemmed in by the uncouth soldiery, who, undisturbed, make sport of His shame and misery. Could He not have hindered this?—Of course. But His wish was to humble Himself to the uttermost. That is the spirit of Christ—a hunger and thirst for humility, for degradation and ignominy before mankind. *Learn of me. Live my life with me. . . .*

How He humbled Himself on the cross, between the two

criminals! In those days there was no more dishonorable death than that of the cross. It was the death of outcasts; and precisely this was the death He chose, consciously and of His own free will—this death and no other. "He humbled himself and became obedient unto death, even the death of the cross," in voluntary obedience to the Father. *Learn of me. Live my life with me. . . .*

Humility is a virtue of Christ. He, the body, must live His life on in the limbs. Hence our lives cannot really be anything but lives of humility, obedience, or making ourselves small and insignificant. Why humility? Because we are limbs of Christ, reproductions of Christ, because we have been baptized and in Baptism have been lifted up into the life of Christ. So let us live in the full consciousness of our unity with Christ. "I am the vine; you the branches" (Jn 15: 5).

(b) Humility is a prerequisite for every true virtue, every perfection. It is the acknowledgment of our nothingness, our complete dependence on God. We acknowledge the fact that we are nothing, that our whole existence is dependent on Him who *is*. How can such an attitude of spirit and will fail to draw to our souls the pleasure of God? How can He, in His divine love, do less than fill with His grace and strength the soul that comes to Him so trustfully, prayerfully, in all its nothingness? The soul is never more ready for grace than when it is humble. "Suffer little children to come unto me." "He who humbleth himself shall be exalted." "To the humble God giveth grace" (1 Pet 5: 5).

Humility is also the acknowledgment of the might, the greatness, the goodness, wisdom, and mercy of God. "Thou alone art good. Hallowed be Thy name." Such adoration honors God. He cannot withhold His choicest gifts from the soul that humbly worships Him. "He who humbleth himself shall be exalted."

If ever we experience setbacks in our journey toward perfection and sanctity, the fault lies in want of humility. All other virtues rest upon and unfold through humility. Humility is the foundation. A life of faith cannot possibly exist without it, without the surrender of our personal will, without the complete yielding of our human insight and judgment on matters concerning our faith. There is no life of obedience without humility—that is, without the sacrifice, the complete, blind surrender of our own will, our own judgment, our own personal wishes. Nor can we truly love our neighbors unless true humility reigns in our hearts. Only one who is really humble is truly unselfish, ignoring self and self-interest. He alone has the aptitude for generosity, large-heartedness, an aptitude that makes possible a life for Christ and for souls, enduring setbacks, ingratitude, sufferings, self-renunciation. Where there is no humility there can be but little love.

Only the humble man can become truly a man of prayer. Prayer is an acknowledgment of personal unimportance, personal nothingness, complete dependence on God and, at the same time, an acknowledgment of the greatness, the goodness, and the love of God toward His creature, His child. Who, then, is in a better frame of mind to pray than the humble man? Only he will show true gratitude regarding everything the day brings as a gift of God and converting every experience, every impression, into a prayer, an act of appreciation, of love, of trust in God, of constant awareness of living in God and the divine Savior. "God gives grace to the humble"—particularly the grace of prayer and the spirit of prayer. The humble man, conscious of his insufficiency, his dependence, his nothingness, is a man of unshakable trust in God. He knows how to subject himself blindly, without reserve or criticism, to his elders and superiors, entirely relinquishing his own wish and will. He knows how to bow quietly, with complete surrender and patience to whatever God may send him, especially through the medium of other people or through the untoward events we all have to face. In the absence of humility our inner life becomes unreal, a sham and a delusion. That is where observance of the com-

mandments becomes twisted into phariseeism; where penitence becomes exhibitionism; where even humility turns
into hypocrisy, virtue into self-assertion. Only on the soil of
true humility can genuine Christian virtue grow.

(c) "Learn of me, for I am meek and humble of heart, and
you shall find rest to your souls" (Mt 11: 29). God has given a
wonderful promise to the humble: *peace*. Who does not seek
peace of heart? And who finds it? He who is humble. "Four
things," says the author of *The Imitation of Christ,* "bring the
soul great peace. First, always to do the will of others rather
than our own; secondly, rather to have less than more;
thirdly, always to seek the lowest place and be submissive;
fourthly, wishing and praying that God's will be done completely. A man who leads his life on these lines is on the right
path for inner peace" (book III, chap. 23). That is the precise
aim and attitude of the humble soul.

There is no man more calm under circumstances of priva-
tion and unpleasantness, of neglect, offense, annoyance of all
kinds, than he who has ceased to be self-seeking—the kind
of man who no longer wants his own way but submits in
everything to the will of God. Such a man acknowledges his
own nothingness. He recognizes himself as a sinner and repeats a thousand times: "I have earned more than has be-
fallen me." This wipes away every shadow of discontent and
criticism, of impatience, of murmuring against God, against
circumstances.

★   ★   ★

LET US examine ourselves earnestly on the questions: How
much have I learned from the Savior? To what extent do I
practice His virtue of humility? To what extent does the
spirit of humility live in me, in my will, and in my actions?

Earnestly we beseech the Lord that His spirit of humility
may be confirmed in us. We only live with Him in spirit to
the extent that we are filled with His spirit of humility. This
is the only soil on which Christian virtues will flourish.

If a religious community, a family, a convent, were to learn from our Savior how to be humble, would that not be paradise on earth, a land of peace, of joy, of indestructible bliss?

13. *Humility*

PART 2

> *Lord teach me thy paths.*
> PSALM 25: 4

THERE IS quite a distance to travel before we who are related by nature to the Pharisee are transformed into the publican—before we become the man who knows his insignificance and helplessness, his total dependence on God and grace, feeling his inner corruption and unworthiness deeply, recognizing and acknowledging it and desiring only to be regarded and treated by others for what he really is. There are penetrating roots in our human nature that resist humility and humiliation. Even where we recognize our insignificance we do not care to adjust ourselves to this self-knowledge. There are many Christians who lead a life of piety and yet keep the spirit of the world firmly entrenched in their hearts; self-love and pride have settled there. So much so that we often, almost without knowing it, share the low esteem in which Christian humility is held. How can we wonder, then, that we find so many shortcomings in Christian families and communities nowadays. The harm lies at the very root.

The kingdom of God rests on justice and truth. Turning away from God through pride, the soul of all sin, is the greatest offense we can commit against Him. It must be stopped. How?—Through humble submission to God in everything. This submission entails humility. The great lie, the origin of all sin, is self-elevation, the spirit that produced autonomy and self-glorification and gives them the status of life principles. This lie must be overcome by humility. Humility is truth. It forces us to give love of God and our neighbor their proper place, as we are commanded to do.

I. OUR PART OF THE WORK

(a) The first factor in the battle for the virtue of humility is the quality of our belief. Faith is the root of all true Christian virtue, the foundation stone of supernatural law and the starting point of our salvation. Faith is also the necessary preliminary to Christian humility, the soil in which it finds its sustenance. In the spirit of faith we arrive at a deeper appreciation of the nature of God. Little by little, an overwhelming idea of the greatness of God, of His holiness, justice, beneficence, and love, must ripen in our soul—an idea so all-embracing that all human conceptions of greatness pale before it.

This conception of God must become an integral part of our being; not only our minds but our bodies, our whole strength, must be caught up in it. It must absorb us completely and never leave us by day or by night. It must be a resplendent light forever leading us, so brilliantly illuminating all that we encounter—mankind, things, ourselves, even the attributes of God—that we see them with totally different eyes. It must become a spontaneous habit to thank Him constantly for all that we are and all that we receive, moment by moment. It must amount to a perpetual and blissful awareness of our dependence on God in the ordering of our everyday existence as well as in the economy of our spiritual life. . . . God immanent in great things and in small. Ever more deeply and joyfully we must realize that we of ourselves are nothing and can do nothing; God is the center and core of our being, all-in-all. Out of this new knowledge of God our prayer grows; we never tire of thanking Him, of singing His praises, of serving Him in a spirit of gratitude.

We arrive at this state by the intensity of our faith. The holy liturgy with its prayers and its offerings, especially the Psalms (which we recite daily), shows us the way. It is not difficult to enter into the spirit of veneration when we allow the liturgy to permeate our whole being. We fall at the feet of the Almighty in humble surrender, lauding His greatness, His wisdom, His justice. "Thou alone art holy; Thou alone, the All Highest." A clear and childlike perception of God, the Eternal: it is precisely here that moderns so often fail. We are too big ourselves to appreciate the greatness of God. We cannot muster up the awe and reverence that are God's due. The smaller God grows in our estimation, the more we make gods of ourselves, barring the progress of Christian humility. "Lord, teach us Thy ways."

In the spirit of faith we are permitted to penetrate the mysteries of the Savior. The stronger the faith with which we approach the Person of our Lord, the more we are able to understand the inner meaning of His life: in the lap of His Virgin Mother, His birth in Bethlehem, His childhood, His quiet life in Nazareth, His ministry, His sufferings and Passion, as we recite them in the sorrowful mysteries of the Rosary and make the pilgrimage of the fourteen Stations of the Cross, and His life in the tabernacle of the altar. Through these mysteries our Lord opens for us the road to humility. In our prayers and meditations we progress along that road. But still the results are meager. Why? We do not bring enough intensity to our devotions. The eye of faith does not penetrate deeply enough. We lack the living faith through which our Lord would let His mysteries do their work in us. We hurry from practice to practice, from prayer to prayer; but they are brittle superficialities. "Teach me, O Lord, Thy ways." Increase, deepen our faith. How otherwise can we truly attain the virtue of humility?

Faith enables us to recognize our nothingness both in our

natural lives and in our state of grace. "What hast thou that thou hast not received?" (1 Cor 4: 7). "It is God who worketh in you, both to will [good] and to accomplish, according to His goodwill" (Phil 2: 13). What credit, therefore, can I honestly give myself? If He did not give me grace, how could I conceive a single good thought, strive for any good object, wish or do any good? We are unutterably more dependent on Him, on His work in us, than we can possibly guess or understand. "What hast thou that thou didst not receive?"—Not a single thought, not a single good decision, not one step or a hand's turn. "Not that we are sufficient to think anything of ourselves, as of ourselves; but our sufficiency is from God" (2 Cor 3: 5). Faith emphatically teaches us: without God we can do nothing, not even pray. "Of himself a man has only untruth and sin. Whatever he possesses in truth and righteousness [virtue, holiness], he draws from a well which we must all seek in this wilderness of our life on earth, in order that we may not faint on the way." And again: "The branches of the vine possess nothing that they do not receive from their life in Him" (Council of Orange). These statements of faith are so many signposts to humility of spirit, of will, and of action. All that is asked of us is that we hold fast, with deep contrition, to our strong faith.

In the spirit of faith we acknowledge and confess our unworthiness before God and our fellow man. We humbly recognize our daily failings, faults, imperfections, shortcomings, perversions, infidelities. What are we?—Sinners, every one of us; prone to sin; full of blindness, frailty, selfishness, haughtiness, corruption. This despite ample divine grace and many excellent examples, good reading, good advice, prayer, and meditation; despite the sacraments and possibly daily Communion. How much reason we have to stand, as the publican in the Gospel did, in the farthest corner, striking our breast and crying: "Lord, have mercy on me, a sinner." How much reason to rank ourselves with the lowest in our homes, in our clothing, in the treatment we expect! How much reason to be meek in our behavior, our attitude, and our speech. Every reason in the world to defer to others, to rate them higher than ourselves, and to submit humbly to injustice and disregard. "By my sins I have merited no better."

In a spirit of faith we surrender ourselves inwardly and outwardly to the will and the commandments of God. We bow in submission to God's representatives here on earth—to our parents, our elders, and our superiors, to clerical authorities, and to those who govern our mundane affairs. We become, like our Lord, obedient unto death, without murmuring, without contradiction, without criticism or discontent, with an upright desire to abide by the laws laid down. In the spirit of faith, every duty, every direction, every rule and order of the authorities is God's will and therefore holy.

(b) Our part of the work also calls for constant and earnest prayer. "Ask, and you shall receive" (Jn 16: 24). The spirit of faith, on which humility rests, is itself a great divine grace. In prayer we confirm our high regard for the virtue of humility. At the same time we acknowledge in prayer that we cannot give ourselves this virtue. In prayer we confess our own helplessness, bowing humbly before God. "He that humbleth himself shall be exalted." Therefore, prayer has an indispensable function in our efforts to acquire the virtue of humility.

2. GOD'S PART IN THE WORK

The bulk of the work, however, is done by God. "Unless the Lord build the house, they labor in vain that build it" (Ps 126: 1). He does not leave us to our own devices. He steps in and works with all his might to heal us of self-conceit, pride, self-inflation. He is a wonderful teacher. He works tirelessly on us, that we may learn to be small and humble, to love humility as our Savior loved and sought it.

(a) To this end God calls us daily to Holy Communion. He uses the Blessed Sacrament to fill us with the spirit of His divine Son, so that our thoughts and judgments, our wishes and endeavors, may become Christlike, perfect. Jesus Christ is the spirit of humility, of humble submission to the Father in all things. It is impossible to receive regular Communion worthily without entering more and more into the Christ-spirit of humility. It is equally true that we are not receiving the Eucharist worthily if we do not derive from it a deeper sense of humility, a deeper appreciation of those who are humble. "By their fruits ye shall know them."

(b) God works unceasingly on us to this end. Our part is simply to submit, offering ourselves, so that He may do with us whatever He wishes, as He wishes: through Himself, through conditions, experiences, events, environment, the time factor, through other people, and so on. Patiently accepting things as they are, not always wishing those with whom we are obliged to live were quite different sorts of people. Not objecting to things or defying them; on the contrary, accepting with joyful resignation whatever comes. For, after all, nothing befalls us except through the will of God—His all-wise, holy will, His providence.

Herein lies the incentive to acquiescent, loving obedience and gratitude, even for that which may seem bitter and unpleasant to us. It touches us in the most sensitive spot: our own personality, our personal way of looking at things; not for myself, not my wishes or desires, hopes, expectations, not my will or what I consider good—but what Thou wilt in me. Thy will be done; only Thine. That is humility, a complete and utterly silent acceptance of whatever God may send, a joyful surrender to His pleasure; the highest function of our free will, our personality, to merge itself in the great effort of realizing at this present moment the humility and obedience of our Lord on the Mount of Olives. "Father, if thou wilt, remove this chalice from me; but yet not my will but thine be done" (Lk 22: 42). This calls for intensive faith.

We have, first of all, to accept the many unpleasant and

even painful occurrences, accidents, and "acts of God" that crop up in every life: circumstances, difficulties, oppositions, hindrances—in fact, everything that goes against our wishes, everything that on purely natural grounds would arouse our anger, everything we should like to annihilate. We have to accept these things because God ordained them, because He permitted them to befall us, because it is His wish that we should bear them for His own good ends. With these trials, which seem so puzzling to us, He is daily, hourly, determining the pattern of our lives. "I am the Lord." He decides. He indicates the way. I have only to bow to His wishes, to fall in with His will. In this way He schools me to be meek and humble. "I say to thee, when thou wast younger, thou didst gird thyself, and didst walk where thou wouldst. But when thou shalt be old, thou shalt stretch forth thy hands, and another shall gird thee, and lead thee whither thou wouldst not" (Jn 21: 18). "I am the Lord."

In the second place, we have to accept the fact that our life has been full of sin. God permitted it, because through sin He can bring us to salvation. We repent, yes. But, all the same, we subject ourselves humbly to the acknowledgment of having sinned, proclaiming ourselves sinners, and in the spirit of deepest contrition cry *mea culpa, mea maxima culpa.* Falling into sin makes the proud man angry with himself: he grieves at the weakness that causes him to fall over and over again. But the meek soul makes even its shame a reason for abasement before God, an act of humble repentance, an incentive to draw closer, in trust and utter submission, to Him alone who can raise us out of sin and guard us against it in future—the way of humility.

In the third place, we must accept the daily disappointments we experience in our inner life—our temptations, our lack of persistence, our disturbing first thoughts and emotions, our imperfections, our weaknesses, our helplessness, our failure to concentrate in prayer, our blindness and stupidity, our want of insight, irresolution in carrying out the promptings of conscience and inspiration, the foundering of our good intentions. If these things make us angry, if they surprise, confuse, or depress us, it is a sure sign that our pride has not yet been overcome. No, we must humble ourselves and bow in acquiescence. "Yea, Father; for so hath it seemed good in thy sight" (Mt 11: 26). Good that I should recognize once again how worthless I am. "Thy will be done."

Finally, we must accept outward humiliation: well-meant as well as destructive criticism from others, unjust judgment, ill-treatment, undeserved demotion, unmerited blame, slander, calumny, accusations of all sorts, trouble caused by our own awkwardness, mistakes that touch our honor and our good name (though we have nothing we can accuse ourselves of in connection with them). Behind all these things that are so hard to bear, our Father, our Savior, stands, showing us the way to humble submission, complete surrender to His guidance, His will. Nothing happens by chance. The hand of God is in all.

Lord, teach me Thy ways! Very few lovingly follow Jesus in His humility. Most people are content with paying lip service to this virtue. If we are called upon to endure a personal affront, how hot and angry we become! Even those who lead a devout life rarely relish going short of their due, and how they object to being ill-used! They dislike being dependent upon others or being regarded as servants; they want to be masters. Yet humility is more valuable than any success or high place we may achieve in the world.

"Progress and perfection lie in submitting thyself with thy whole heart to the divine pleasure, offering thyself up and seeking nothing for thyself, either in great things or in small, either in time or eternity, weighing all things with the scale of righteousness and giving thanks to Me for both the good and the adverse circumstances thou art called upon to encounter. When thou art strong, and so securely anchored in trust [to God] that thou art ready for even greater sufferings, that thou no longer desirest to justify thyself and deemest all

My ordinances righteous, then thou art on the road to peace" (*The Imitation of Christ*).

★   ★   ★

To WHAT extent does the spirit of faith live in me? How far have I progressed in true appreciation of the might of God? How deeply have I entered into the mystery of Jesus' humility? What is the measure of my conscious unworthiness in the sight of God? Exactly how much submission do I bring to my Maker, letting Him do His holy work in me, and humbly accepting all that He sends to try me?

I have need of much prayer for strength in all these things. Only God's grace can heal me of my pride. Only those who pray can find the way to humility and, with complete self-renunciation, take it.

14. *Christian Prayer*

PART I

Lord, teach me to pray.
LUKE II: I

THERE IS something very striking about the prayer of our Lord. He prayed in His earthly life; He still prays in our midst in the Blessed Sacrament of the Altar. He prays, offers Himself up, gives thanks, praises petitions, and atones perpetually, day and night. His prayer is so pure, so heartfelt, so inestimably valuable, that the Father's eye rests with eternal pleasure on this worshipper, and He accepts His prayer with constant delight. Once, our Lord spent some time in prayer, and, as He finished, one of His disciples said, "Lord, teach us to pray" (Luke 11: 1), for he was so much impressed with the sight of our Lord at prayer. Give us light and give us grace to absorb the mystery of prayer, so that we may learn to lead a life of prayer, according to the example Thou gavest us.

1. THE REASON FOR PRAYER

(a) "All things are created for the purpose of prayer" (St. Francis de Sales), so that they may glorify the Creator, recognizing Him as their starting point and objective, and in deep humility and submission chorus His praises. Creatures that have no power of reason do this by merely existing. By the very fact that they have been called into being out of nothing they proclaim the Creator's power, wisdom, and goodness, which gave them life and sustains it, directing their being and their functions so that they may fulfill their purpose in the created universe.

"All things are created for the purpose of prayer." If this applies to creatures without reasoning power, how much more it must be true of man. For man has been put on this earth so that he may consciously know his Creator as the beginning and end of his being; so that he may extol God's greatness, might, wisdom, and beneficence, so that he may yield his whole being in loving surrender to his Maker, thanking Him, praising Him—that is, so that he may *pray*. Prayer is a requirement that springs directly from the recognition of man's dependence, in all that he is and has, on his Creator.

(b) But for us Christians, prayers go beyond this to other, quite supernatural, causes. We Christians pray:

(1) Because, thanks to our salvation through Christ, we have become children of God. "God sent his Son, . . . that we [all men, Jews, Gentiles] might receive the adoption of sons [children of God]. And because you are sons, God hath sent the Spirit of his Son into your hearts, crying, Abba, Father" (Gal 4: 4–6). The same Apostle writes: "You have received the spirit of adoption of sons, whereby we cry, Abba, Father" (Rom 8: 15). A new spirit lives in us, the baptized, the spirit of children loving the Father through the Holy Spirit in us, which impels us, from within, to turn toward God and hail Him "Father."

In this one word, "Father," we voice our faith, our childlike trust, our surrender, our love, our contrition, our petition, our will to live for Him, to yield ourselves in everything to His holy will for us. Our Christian prayer, therefore, is not just the expression of purely natural man's relation with God who created him. We come to Him in our prayers rather as children to their heavenly Father, to praise, bless, and love Him, to petition Him for the help we require. We do not forget that we are His creatures but our prayer is not based on this; it is based rather on our dignity and our position as children of God. Filled with childlike reverence, we approach the Father in the confidence that He extends to us His fatherly beneficence and that we can yield ourselves to Him trustfully, with heartfelt love. Our prayer therefore has its roots in the fact of our being children of God, i.e., that we are in sanctifying grace, which proceeds from the Holy Spirit. It is the act, not of natural man, but of grace.

(2) Because by virtue of Baptism we are in Christ Jesus; we are branches of Christ, the vine, whose life we share, because it flows in us, just as the branches share the life of the vine. We can offer our prayer—that is, our address of love to the Father—only insofar as we are in Christ, sharing His life. But the life of Christ is a complete and loving surrender to the Father; His life is turned in love completely Godward. In other words, it is a life of prayer. Thanks to our life in Christ, we, too, are caught up in this loving surrender to the Father. With Him, in Him, and through Him we speak the words of love: "Hallowed be Thy Name; Thy kingdom come; Thy will be done." With Him, in Him, and through Him we petition with childlike trust: "Give us this day our daily bread. Forgive us our trespasses. Deliver us from evil." Thereby we link ourselves in prayer with our Lord Jesus Christ, speaking His words of love reverently with Him.

Our prayer is not only the prayer of natural man with his limitations and insignificance; it is actually the prayer of Christ, who prays in us to the Father. Our own inadequate prayer is carried up and ennobled by the dignity and the power of Christ. "He that abideth in me, and I in him, the same beareth much fruit" (Jn 15: 5). He who prays in Me, and I in him, his prayers shall be fruitful. "I live, now not I, but Christ liveth in me" (Gal 2: 20). I pray, yet, actually, not I: Christ prays in me. The more deeply we live in Christ, sharing His life, the more fruitful our prayers are and the better they do their work.

Christ is the great worshipper. As the eternal Son of God, as the Logos, He is the Word in which God expressed the glory of His Person and His divine riches and from which the full splendor of the Father radiates. He is "the brightness of his glory, the figure of his substance" (Heb 1: 3), the complete image and representation of the greatness of Almighty God; He is the eternal glorification of God the Father. Lovingly, the Son gazes upon the magnificence of the Father, extolling Him in the perpetual hymn of which God alone is completely worthy.

The eternal Word was made man in Christ. This means that the human life of our Lord is also caught up in the laudation of the eternal Word and becomes an eternal hymn of praise, an everlasting prayer, a Word of Love. This exaltation irradiates the whole life of Christ, from the first moment in the womb of the Virgin Mother, in the crib, in the quiet retirement of Nazareth, in His ministry, on the cross, and now in Heaven and in the Sacrament of the Altar—the most perfect exaltation of God, the perfect prayer.

But it is the wish of Christ to extend His life, to extend His prayer. That is why He has shared His life with us in Baptism; that is why He draws us daily to participate in the Mass and to partake of Holy Communion: draws us unto Himself, so that we may pray with deeper reverence, surrender ourselves more completely in His surrender, and unite with Him in prayer and praise. He desires to reproduce His *Gloria Patri* in us, so that it will rise perpetually, everywhere, from thousands of loving hearts in a mighty choir in the community of the Church, in Heaven and on earth.

(3) Because prayer, petition, is absolutely necessary to us. "Not that we are sufficient to think anything of ourselves, as of ourselves, but our sufficiency is from God," writes the Apostle. God "worketh in you to will and to accomplish, according to his goodwill." In spite of all our good intentions, all our strivings, we are simply not able by our own natural powers to overcome the evils that seek to trip us up, the

temptations besetting us; nor can we do the good we wish to do. Yet the same Apostle tells us emphatically: "I can do all things . . ." (Phil 4: 13); everything—even the greatest and most difficult things; everything—"in him that strengtheneth me."

But whom does God strengthen, to whom does He give power and grace?—To the one who prays. "Ask, and it shall be given you" (Mt 7: 7). If you do not pray, you shall not receive; if you pray little, you will receive little; if you pray much, you will receive much. That is the law. God wants to give us His grace; but His will is that we shall pray before we receive it. Of course, all good works also bring us nearer to God and insure us a corresponding growth in healing grace. But there is one especially effective way of attaining grace, and that is through prayer. It is the medium that at all times comes easiest to hand. It is the first medium the soul reaches for in its upward impulse; it is the last medium the soul turns to when death knocks at the door. It is one of the most powerful and effective mediums for uniting us with God and putting grace within our reach. "Ask, and it shall be given you." For "God giveth grace to the humble." In the prayer of petition we acknowledge our nothingness, our utter helplessness, because of which we are all dependent upon God's grace. In the prayer of petition we recognize and acknowledge the greatness, the power, and the beneficence of God, and in so doing direct the flood of our veneration into our prayer, glorifying and honoring God. We Christians pray:

(4) Because we are children of the Holy Church, and the Church needs worshippers. Herself the "praying Church," she lives for worship—praying to God, praising Him, glorifying Him. In loving surrender, ever ready to work for God's interests and suffer for them, if need be, the Church keeps her thoughts, her heart, her attention unswervingly on God, united in spirit with the great worshipper, Christ, with whom she is so intimately linked. She prays in Heaven, she prays in Purgatory, she prays here on earth: "We bless thee,

we praise thee, we worship thee." When here on earth a congregation of worshippers grows tired or is called to other duties, instantly another takes up the prayer. Day and night,
round the entire earth, the Church prays unceasingly.

The Church prays in the persons of her priests, to whom
it entrusts the breviary, with the strict injunction never to let
a day pass, to the end of their lives, without offering up the
stipulated prayer of the Church. The Church prays in her
numerous religious orders, members of which are handed
their breviary on making their profession. Day and night,
wherever there are priests and religious orders, worshippers
kneel around the tabernacle, united in their prayers of love,
gratitude, petition, and atonement, with the sacred High
Priest, Christ—a pure, holy, inestimably fruitful worship
with Christ, "through Christ our Lord."

The Church prays vicariously for so many of her children
who have forgotten how to pray or who are hindered from
doing so. She prays for many who do not want to be her children and who stand outside, far removed from their Mother,
rapidly perishing of misery and hunger. It prays vicariously
for the whole world, for all who are in need, tired, tempted,
oppressed, or in spiritual danger.

The world, so far from God, does not pray. It seeks relief in
broken cisterns (Jer 2: 13), in the stepping-up of human
achievement, in learning, in ever more daring enterprises, in
the destruction of the past, in technical progress, in boundless effort for wealth and well-being, yes, and in turning away
from God and Christ, in combat against the Church of
Christ, in encouraging unbelief, in making gods of men and
false gods of work, success, money, the nation, the State. The
world needs no God, no light, no outside help; it is sufficient
unto itself. That is also why it needs no prayer. In consequence of this, the Church's task, our task, is all the greater—
the task of prayer. In prayer we must make good all that is
lacking; praying, we must do penance and atone; praying, ask
for forgiveness and grace, especially in these days of material,

spiritual, and moral need. What can save the world? Not learning, not technical knowledge, not politics, not human power. The only thing that can save us is the mercy of God and His grace, and this can be attained only through prayer. The healing of the world lies in prayer. The need of the world today cries out for praying souls. Souls willing to link up with the Church, with Christ, in a united, Heaven-rending *Kyrie eleison*, in an incessant "Hallowed be Thy name."

"Pray without ceasing." "Ask and ye shall receive." "We believe that no one can be saved without God's help, and that no one asks His help but the one who prays" (St. Augustine). "All saints became blessed and holy because they prayed. All who have been lost were lost because they did not pray. Had they prayed persistently they would have been saved" (St. Alphonsus Liguori). "No one is more powerful than the man who prays" (St. Chrysostom). The strength of the Church lies in the prayers of Christians.

2. THE PURPOSE OF CHRISTIAN PRAYER

What do we desire when we pray?—In the last analysis, nothing but the unity of our will with God's, the loving surrender of our heart to God. We desire ardently to be with the Father, near to Him, doing homage to Him with our love.

There are two ways in which we can contact God and achieve this unity: through our spirit and through our will. The spirit achieves unity with God through our thinking about His presence or His various perfections, His providence, His works; or in reflecting on one of the mysteries, a better understanding of which brings us nearer to God. But it would be a great mistake to conclude that this method of approach to God constitutes prayer. Meditation is only a means—a preparation for prayer in its proper sense, which, briefly, is a loving union of heart and will with God.

(a) In this union of the will with God, we desire, above all, to adore, to give ourselves with all our love to God so that He may exercise His majesty and might and love in us without any hindrance. Our surrender in its awe and love must be so complete that, inwardly and outwardly, He is "all-in-all" (1 Cor 15: 28). Adoration, loving homage, is the real inwardness, the soul, of prayer, even prayer of petition. First, we pray "Hallowed be Thy name," the adoration, the approach to God; then, the much wider application: "Give us this day our daily bread. Forgive us our trespasses." Worshipping love, glorification of God, is the goal to which all other forms of prayer are subordinated.

God and the glorification of God first and foremost. . . . That is why it is a mistake to regard prayer simply as a means to spiritual well-being or to self-perfection, thus giving priority to the service for our own soul over glorification of God; as if the saving of the soul—i.e., of man—were the highest and final goal of creation! It is far more correct to say that our soul's healing is also a part of adoration, the glorification of God. We strive constantly for spiritual progress only so that we may worship God more perfectly and, therefore, that the homage we bring to Him may be more worthy of His divine majesty.

Adoration and thanksgiving are most intimately linked. We know—and each day brings us further proof of it—for how much we are in duty bound to be grateful. Everything we are and have, either by nature or by grace, comes to us from the beneficence and the mercy of God. Where should we be if He had not from the beginning loved us so much that He decided to create us, to give us all the aptitudes, talents, and powers we possess? Where should we be if He had not in His endless mercy sent His only-begotten Son to tear us from the clutches of sin, hell, and the devil, turning us into God's children and making available to us the inexhaustible grace that is constantly at our command? Consider the love He showers upon us daily, hour by hour; grace without measure and without end; the grace of enlightenment, of inner prompting, of strength against evil—power for good, courage to preserve virtue. So we experience an imperative need to give thanks to our greatest Benefactor—the grateful, loving assent of our will to all that comes to us from God.

A third object we have when we pray is that of returning to the Father, whom by our sins we have so deeply offended, in a spirit of repentance and true resolution to make amends. It is unfortunately true that we have all disobeyed His commandments, opposed His will; that we have set our own moods and fancies above His wishes. What can we do, faced with so many affronts to God, except pronounce our sincere *mea culpa*, weeping over our sins and expressing our readiness to do penance? So we come in contrition to the Father and await the word of forgiveness. We recognize and glorify Him in this as the Lord of mercy.

A fourth purpose of Christian prayer is petition. In petition we turn to God's might and abundance, which bestow on us the grace and help we need. In this form of prayer we demonstrate our faith in the love our Father bears toward us, His children, and at the same time express our dependence on God's bounty, our need, our complete helplessness apart from Him who is our constant help. In the prayer of petition we recognize that He, as our Father, divinely desires to take us, His children, up into His life, offering us the abundance of His riches; that He is only too ready to give us all the help we need to attain the Christian goal of eternal life. We lift our hands and hearts to the Father in prayer and remember the many others who have asked us to pray for them, those for whom we are bound in duty to pray, and those who are averse to us, who do us harm, who hate us. In the prayer of petition we honor God's omnipotence, His beneficence, and His love. We yield ourselves entirely to this might, this goodness, this love of God. Thus, not even in our prayer of petition are we entirely preoccupied with our need. We do not halt in the act of asking; we throw ourselves upon God with our cry for help and at the same time glorify Him with our trust and adoration.

Our prayer of petition is not to be regarded as a plea to God to change His mind or alter His plans or intentions. We should pray to God in the conviction that, in His fatherly love, He has from the beginning taken up our prayer and fitted it into the plan of His divine providence. In this way our petition acquires meaning and efficiency even though it is true that God's will is absolute and unalterable.

(b) Whatever rises to God in the form of prayer descends again to the worshipper as grace and blessing. If the purpose of Christian prayer is in the first place adoration of God—the goal of our life—it is, in the second place, an incomparable means for building up a good Christian life. St. John Eudes did not exaggerate when he described prayer as "a matter so weighty that the earth that bears us, the air we breathe, the bread we eat, the heart that beats in our breast are less important in the leading of a human life" (*Royaume*, 2, 11). All earnest, genuine prayer transforms us and makes us holier, more Godlike. It loosens the ties that bind us to inordinate affection for earthly things, so far as those are opposed to our surrender to God.

Because prayer is a surrender to God, an elevation of the soul, it weakens the power of self-love, our passions, and evil inclinations. When we pray, we penetrate ever more deeply into the divine and recognize more clearly the questionable value of earthly possessions and enjoyments. Thus prayer leads to, and furthers, our unity with God. In prayer our spirit touches God and becomes increasingly illuminated by the light of God. The will becomes increasingly bound up with God's holy will. The heart is more and more attracted to the eternal goodness and love of the Father in Heaven, captivated and filled by the divine love, which is actually God Himself. Thus true prayer makes a new man of the worshipper, enabling him more and more to share God's life.

Just as Christian prayer guards our inner life, so too it has a tremendous influence on our outer life and activities. That is the secret of the fruitful results achieved by the saints. They prayed, earnestly and often. Prayer gave them the strength for their self-sacrifice, the painstaking performance of their duties, for their tireless service, and their heroic deeds. Work and prayer, activity and contemplation, go well together and support one another.

All our prayers—our adoration, veneration, petition, thanksgiving—return to us from God as blessings, fruitful in help and spiritual growth. They lead to a constantly deeper and more intense unity with God. So it is perfectly true that prayer is the nourishment of the Christian soul; it is the very breath of the soul. Whoever stops praying stops breathing, living. Alternatively, if a Christian wishes to live a vital life of faith, seeking earnestly to attain perfection with the help of God's grace, he can do so only by prayer, simultaneously praying and breathing in divine grace, and, in it, giving himself back to God.

Still, the ultimate aim of prayer is not man's inner growth nor service to his soul. We hallow ourselves with our prayers only so that we may glorify God more, adoring and loving Him. The purer, the richer, the holier we are through prayer, the more our adoration becomes pleasing to God. So prayer aids our inner growth but that in its turn increases our veneration, the sole purpose for which we were created.

Therefore, Christian prayer should be for us something great and holy. Is it not the greatest honor that could have been bestowed on us poor human beings, that we are permitted to pray, that we have direct access to our Father in Heaven, that we are actually allowed to speak to Him? And that He condescends in His love and goodness to hear us and, when we weep, lovingly embraces us?

★ ★ ★

How thankful we must be that we can pray!
What efforts we must make to pray worthily!
How we must prize and love Christian prayer!
"Lord, teach us to pray!"

15. *Christian Prayer*

PART 2

The truth shall make you free.
JOHN 8: 32

THERE IS much ignorance and confusion regarding prayer; and there are also many false impressions. As a result, some people tend to make heavy going of it. This of course robs prayer of all joy, and after a time even the courage to pray disappears; one simply grows tired of praying, having completely lost trust in the power of prayer. Much of this confusion may be traced to a false conception of prayer. We are not quite clear as to what prayer really is. So, our first step should be to try to grasp the essential properties of good prayer.

Many people are quite convinced that they are not praying worthily unless they are inwardly gripped and held. No distraction of any kind, no matter how involuntary or unsought, must interrupt their concentration, otherwise the prayer is useless. Others believe that it is impossible to pray unless they are in the right mood. Still others imagine that when, because of exhaustion, tiredness, sickness, weakness, or outer disturbance, they get no satisfaction—feeling cold, comfortless, and empty after their devotions—their prayers have been in vain. There are many who work themselves up into an excited state over prayer, which misfires, and then they discard what they have already offered, starting over again and again, until they persuade themselves at last that they have done their best and leave it at that. So, with admirable intentions, many people worry themselves unnecessarily and often tumble into more and more blunders and difficulties.

Hence the question: What is prayer? What do we need in order to pray sincerely and worthily, to make our prayer pleasing to God?

First we must distinguish two kinds of prayer; the finite act of prayer, interrupted and restarted; and the state of constant prayer, that is, the habitual attitude of the soul that has one prayer it holds perpetually, without ceasing.

I. OCCASIONAL PRAYER

(a) What makes the *Gloria Patri* a true prayer, pleasing to God?

From the spiritual point of view prayer is not, fundamentally, an intellectual exercise, a matter of reciting words with complete understanding of their inner meaning or of mentally debating those words. The nature of prayer is really in no way dependent on reasoning or even on such concentration that a momentary and involuntary wandering of thought automatically cancels out the intention. Nor is prayer a flight of fancy in which one conjures up images as, for instance, that of the Savior, or of the Blessed Virgin, or of some picture inspired by Sacred Scripture. Still less is prayer a matter of stirring up pious feelings. This does not imply that intellect, imagination, and emotion have no part in prayer. But, valuable and necessary as they are, they must be regarded only as preparations for prayer. They do not affect the nature of prayer and are not prayers in themselves. A prayer can be worthy and pleasing to God without a single one of these things.

Prayer could be described as an inner urge inspired by the Holy Spirit and resulting in a voluntary, supernatural act, i.e., an act in which the child of God turns with awe and love to the Father, surrendering himself lovingly to Him, worshipping Him in the unity of love. We are actually impelled toward the Father by love, which came to us through the Holy Spirit when Baptism made us one with Christ and conferred on us sonship by adoption. Since we received "the Spirit of adoption, whereby we cry 'Abba, Father'" (Rom 8: 15), our soul's impulse is to turn Godward, calling Him by that name, the name that is at once a term of endearment and a prayer—the word that not only implies childlike trust but also adoration, praise, gratitude, admiration for God's greatness, beauty, and majesty. It implies not only love but also submission, awe.

In its innermost quality, prayer is an act of love. The more a prayer expresses love (i.e., the more the worshipper rises above limited personal love to divine love, which is complete fulfillment) the more perfect the act becomes. Love can never be too often expressed, even when the recipient knows already that it exists. Hence, whenever love of God prompts us to pray, we have the blissful assurance that God, who lives in the depths of our being through our oneness with His only begotten Son, hears our prayer and graciously accepts it—all the more so because we are joined in our prayer, in loving surrender to the Father, by our indwelling Savior Himself. We pray "through Christ our Lord," and as members of His body we are most intimately linked with His perpetual adoration. What immense power this lends to our prayers!

In the act of prayer we rise above our mortal selves and approach the Father, offering ourselves to Him, completely subject to His intentions and interests. As a mark of this subjection we come with folded hands upraised. Ages ago, the vassal in the same way placed his hands into those of his liege lord as a sign of humble submission and sworn allegiance.

(b) What do we wish to attain by our prayers?

What is the object of praying?—Primarily, union with God, who actually lives in the depths of our soul and who draws us to Him in order that we may share His life. Praying, we yield to the magnetic force of the Holy Trinity and let it do its work in us. This unifies us with God and gradually transforms all our thoughts, judgments, intentions, and actions, making them purer, holier, more Godlike. If our prayer does not gradually draw us away from earthly things, from personality and human errors of the past, if it does not convert us more and more to Christ's ways, then it is no true prayer.

At the same time, in as much as unity with God—God's love—is the object of prayer, while it achieves this, it also serves the greatest of all ends—that is, the adoration, the glorification, of God. The more we liberate and bless ourselves in prayer, the more perfectly we honor and adore our Maker.

2. PRAYER AS A CONDITION OF SOUL

The act of prayer is a passing act. It is not the last word in prayer. It is a way to prayer as condition of soul—that is to say, a continuous state of prayer, nourished and strengthened by acts of prayer and necessarily requiring acts of prayer. It is a matter of decisive importance from the Christian standpoint that we should arrive at a state of constant prayer. Clearly, when we speak of a state of prayer, we do not mean spoken prayer, nor do we mean the inner, so-called contemplative prayer, for it is humanly impossible to commune uninterruptedly with God or to devote ourselves with undivided attention entirely to divine matters.

Prayer as a condition of soul is, more properly speaking, a permanent inner attitude of loving surrender to God, a childlike submission to His divine will and providence in all the affairs of our life. It is a constant attitude of compliance, in which our will completely yields itself to God's wishes for us, to whatever He sends us in the way of tasks, duty, rules, or commandments; ready at all times, no matter what the inconvenience or effort involved, to speak the word of acquiescence. "Hallowed be Thy name. Thy will be done." "Yes, Father, for so hath it seemed good in Thy sight." . . . It is complete non-resistance; constant and cheerful readiness to welcome the difficulties and bitternesses, the mischances, disappointments, sufferings, ill health, that God in His providence sees fit to send us day by day.

A valuable, grace-acquiring state. . . . When our will is completely set in this condition it is almost impossible for us to fall into any error that would be displeasing to God or against our own conscience. We are caught up in an ardent desire to please God more and more, never having any wish to oppose His will and accepting with loving submission from His hands whatever He sends, commands, or recommends, whatever He chooses to take from us.

Prayer as a condition is a silent, continuous merging of our will in God's, coupled with complete readiness on our part to let Him do in us whatever may seem right to His providence and love. It is the prayer of intensity, offering up from our innermost depths, where, through sanctifying grace, the soul is united with the indwelling Holy Trinity. To speak figuratively, it is the perpetual glow out of which in natural evolution flames spark up every now and then. The glow remains, even when the flames are not very quick to make their appearance.

This elevated state of constant prayer, which rests upon surrender to and unity with God, is fed by acts of prayer, which move upon the surface of the soul. It is equally true that these surface prayers are in their turn nourished by the intense, inner state of prayer out of which they grow. This multiplies them, makes them purer, richer, more fruitful, in proportion to the degree of perfection the state of prayer has reached.

(a) In Christian life, the state of constant prayer is of the highest importance. Our daily activities must be entirely re-assessed in the light of intense prayer, for it is to this productive condition of prayer that we owe our spiritual growth and our ability to glorify God. We pray to Him with our labors, with our sacrifices and sufferings; even when we are not thinking of prayer we pray to Him, so long as we offer these acts and sufferings in loving veneration to God and in complete submission to His will. By this attitude we are enabled to "pray without ceasing" (1 Th 5: 17), to "pray always," as our Lord requires of us (Lk 21: 36). We must keep our minds on our work; we cannot be thinking of God the whole time—but we can do our work in such a way that it is in itself an act of prayer. Thanks to our perpetual union with God, in the state of constant prayer, everything we do in submission to His will is to His honor and glory.

Intense prayer is of especial importance when we are dealing with the internal and external difficulties that we sometimes experience in our devotions; for instance, tiredness, headache, boredom, inability to concentrate, outward disturbances, errant thoughts, aridity, reluctance, tediousness, and all the other agitating influences that we cannot master and that are liable to vex us at any time. Through our perpetual readiness to merge our will completely in that of God, who in prayer directs our attention to the cross, we can turn these vexations into prayer. This we do by accepting the failures that attend our efforts despite all good intentions. We admit and accept the fact of our own complete impotence. It is precisely in this act of surrender that we unite our will, if not our spirit, with God's—and that, too, is prayer.

Here we may easily fall into error. We may believe that our prayer is acceptable only when our spirit is directed with lively attention to God. True enough, we pay more attention when our thoughts are not scattered, but this does not mean that in our battle with distractions we fail to make contact with God, provided we submit to His will when He lays the cross of distraction upon us. In obedience to our inner devotional impulse, we do our best to overcome the destructive intruders and, as soon as we become aware of their presence, try hard to recollect ourselves. That is as it should be, but if, despite our well-meant efforts, we cannot succeed in protecting ourselves against distraction, we need not become depressed or even grieve about it, as though we had committed an offense. If only we bow to the cross, that is, to the will of God, by that very act of acquiescence we perform a true act of prayer. The fundamental law of the cross, the law of suffering, applies to prayer as it does to every other aspect of Christian life. We affirm it as we continually repeat our intense surrender to God's will, which grows stronger as it becomes habitual; then the very difficulties that beset us, far from hindering, actually nourish our prayer and bring it nearer to perfection.

It is a comforting reflection that our incapacity simply cannot adversely affect our prayers—provided, of course, that our will is in complete subjection to God's. An act of prayer springing from such an attitude is always devout. For essential devotion lies in the direction of our will. It does not really matter if non-essential elements, such as emotional devotion or a slight admixture of the more sensual part of our nature, are absent from it. Only essential devotion—that is, the correct attitude of will—is absolutely necessary. But the will, which expresses itself in this attitude, leads quite naturally to spiritual awareness of God; and as we increase our strength of will, this awareness increases.

All the same, even when, with complete surrender of our will, we bow meekly to interruptions, and even when, on the outer plane, we do our best to develop concentration, we still may not escape the cross of distraction in prayer. These distractions creep in against our will and without our noticing them. Does our prayer suffer in value and usefulness as a result?—By no means. The will is, and remains, linked with God despite the unsought diversions, and, instead of cutting us off from God, they draw us closer to Him. Our prayer loses nothing in value of essential devotion; on the contrary, by bestirring us to humility, it links us even more intimately with God. Thus the distraction, the difficulty, is converted into a grace.

The more we grasp the essence of Christian prayer the more we free ourselves from the many false conceptions that confuse us. We clearly recognize that everything depends upon the attitude of will, on the subjection of our personal will to the will of God. Praying is actually the desire to pray. It becomes clear to us that we really can pray effectively despite all our incapacity, despite all weaknesses, difficulties, and unsought distractions. We should fully understand that as long as our will in prayer seeks God, only God, and God's will, we truly pray.

(b) One word more remains to be said regarding our prayers to Christ, our supplications to our Blessed Mother and to the saints.

When we pray to Christ we pray in the same sense that we pray to the Father, to the Holy Trinity; for Christ, the Son of God made man, is Himself true God and one with the Father. The essence of prayer to Christ is loving adoration, loving surrender to His Person, His commandments, His holy will. But through Christ we offer our prayers to the Father. Christ the Lord takes the prayer we direct to Him and carries it to the Father. So in our prayer to Christ we pray in, with, and through Him to the Father.

To Mary and the saints we pray not in the sense of adoration—that belongs to the Father and to Christ and to the Holy Spirit alone—but in the sense of religious veneration due to their supernatural superiority. To our Lady we owe a deeper veneration than to the saints, the angels, and all mankind because of the divine favor that gives her precedence over all. If our veneration of our Lady and the saints is not an act of prayer, it is, nevertheless, an attitude of will, which acknowledges the greatness, the grace, the virtue, and the holiness passing beyond Mary and the saints to God Himself, thanking Him in his saints, extolling and glorifying Him with his saints, with their hearts, with their love, and with their surrender to His will. When we turn in trust to our heavenly Mother we do so in the clear realization that she is not our last recourse; we do so because she takes us with her to her Son and through Him to the Father, supplementing our love and our surrender with her own love and making good that which is wanting in us.

★ ★ ★

"IF THOU didst know the gift of God!" (Jn 4: 10), the grace, the sublime power of Christian prayer. . . .

Our Christian prayer has a dynamic force and power immeasurably greater than any human strength. What power has learning, technical skill, even the might of Satan and Hell compared with the potency of human prayer carried to God by Christ Himself? "If thou didst know the gift of God!" . . .

Obviously we ought to value Christian prayer more highly—to rely more on its power—believe more in its power—and especially convince ourselves that, in spite of our human incapacity, we can pray in a manner pleasing to God. When our will is really integrated in the will of God we pray perpetually. Then our whole life is a constant prayer, an endless act of love toward God.

What bliss will be ours when we learn to let the grace of God work in us without let or hindrance: then we shall no longer rely on our own human capacity, even in our prayers.

16. *Inwardness*

Pray without ceasing.
LUKE 21: 36

IN HIS epistle to the Colossians, St. Paul describes the kind of everyday life Christians should lead. "Seek the things that are above, where Christ is sitting at the right hand of the Father. Mind the things that are above, not the things that are upon the earth. For you are dead [unregenerated man]; and your life is hid with Christ in God. Stripping yourselves of the old man with his deeds and putting on the new. . . ."

Especially is it the Christian's duty to give love the foremost place in his daily life. "Bearing with one another . . . if any have a complaint against another. . . . Let the word of Christ dwell in you abundantly in all wisdom: teaching and admonishing one another in psalms, hymns, and spiritual canticles. . . . All whatsoever you do, . . . do all in the name of the Lord Jesus Christ, giving thanks to God" (Col 3: 1–17).

And again: "Continue in prayer and watch in the same with thanksgiving." To the Ephesians he writes: "Redeeming the time, . . . understand what is the will of God. . . . Be ye filled with the Holy Spirit, speaking to yourselves in psalms, and hymns, and spiritual canticles, singing and making melody in your hearts to the Lord. Giving thanks always for all things, in the name of the Lord Jesus Christ, to God the Father" (Eph 5: 16–20). A life of constant gratitude to God, a happy state of trust in God, of incessant living communion with God. That is the Apostle Paul's concept of a Christian life.

It was self-evident to St. Paul and the early Christians that everything they did should be done in the name of Jesus, in an attitude of prayer, and that their hearts should sing with thankfulness to God and gratitude for whatever life might bring them, whether satisfying or trying. They were so filled with God, with faith in the great beneficence they owed to Him, and they saw God and His goodness so clearly in everything, that they felt impelled continually to sing His praises.

We, on the other hand, make heavy weather of a life of true inwardness, of the injunction to "pray without ceasing." Not that we are lacking in good intentions or an upright desire for an intense inner life, for closer unity with God and Christ. It is simply that we do not grasp the meaning of unceasing prayer.

I. THE MEANING OF INWARDNESS

It may be that in olden times people did not find it any problem to convert their everyday activities into constant prayer. They lived more quietly. There was never the tension between worldly turmoil and inner peace that there is today. Nowadays we have to keep our thoughts intent upon our work, on the fulfillment of our duty, on the machine we are minding. Our studies, our profession, our household tasks demand all our concentrated attention. We are normally so taken up with our occupations that for hours at a stretch we can spare no thought for anything else at all, least of all for God. How far we have wandered from St. Paul's ideal, "Sing to the Lord in your hearts!" Hence the question: How can we link up communion with God, the state of constant prayer, of piety and true inwardness, with the irresistible drag of modern life? Or, in other words, of what does true inwardness, conscious and constant communion with God, really consist?

(a) Inner life, communion with God, does not depend simply on the number of religious exercises, spoken prayers, meditations, indulgences, pious readings, and church attendances we can fit into the day. Many people confuse piety—

true inwardness—with pious practices and regard themselves as more and more devout in proportion to the number of these achievements they can chalk up to their credit. When occasionally, through no fault of their own, these good people are forced to curtail their religious exercises, they are loud in lamentation and look upon themselves as already lost—as if practices of piety were piety itself! In reality, a life of Christian inwardness by no means demands an immense prayer output. Neither does it require many hours of ardent praying, meditation, or reflection on God and His mysteries; nor even constant thinking of God, or a succession of mental pictures of God, always close at hand, following us around with His pursuing glance. It does not even require a certain "worked-up" feeling of God's nearness.

(b) True inwardness, conscious union with God, is fundamentally not a matter of thought or mental processes at all, but rather a matter of will. It is not a succession of acts but an attitude, a condition, an endless, unchangeable state of love for God, of trust in God, of complete subjection to God's command and will. Essentially bound up with all this, there should be a constant alertness for the inner voice of God, which makes itself known to us in countless unmistakable ways: promptings, impulses, reminders, warnings, pricks of conscience. Inwardness, a constant state of prayer, does not therefore consist of acts but of a permanent soul-attitude involving the subordination of our will to God's—an attitude grounded in an all-embracing, loving faith that, without effort, habitually sees God and God's will, providence, and love in everything. From this standpoint the soul gratefully, joyfully, even quite naturally yields itself to God's will without the least resistance—throws itself confidently into His loving arms. In all things, in occurrences, duties, and difficulties, as well as in the demands of conscience, it hears God's voice and invitation. Then it answers with a joyful "As it pleases Thee," even if not in acts, then at least in readiness: in its attitude of agreement.

It is completely dead to its own will. Its sole interest is in God and His pleasure.

Our proper attitude to God is one of faith-inspired trust, as we turn with deep reverence and love to our Father. It should consist of a permanent state of yielding with complete willingness to whatever God wills, ever ready to bear any sufferings, sacrifices, burdens, difficulties, or failures He may choose to send us.

In this "state of constant prayer" we do not spend all our time thinking of God; nor do we occupy ourselves with useless and idle thoughts; nor are we continually "saying prayers." The essential thing here is that our will, our heart, is forever turned toward God, happily content to avoid anything that might offend Him and seeking only that which will give Him pleasure.

True inwardness—"prayer without ceasing"—is thus by no means impossible; it is not even particularly difficult to attain. Yet there are very few who achieve it. Why?—Because few possess the faculty necessary for incessant prayer. Anyone who wishes to attain this faculty must give himself entirely and without reserve to God, seeking nothing and asking nothing for himself; for God alone, for His divine pleasure. Complete exclusion of selfishness and self-love is necessary. The soul no sooner surrenders to God than He floods it with a new awareness of His presence. Then begins the germination of true inwardness, which enables the soul to preserve its tranquility amid all the turmoil of daily life so that, in conscious awareness of the indwelling Presence, it can at last pray without ceasing.

(c) So it is that "prayer without ceasing," like all true prayer, requires the complete crossing-out of self—a severance from everything that does not minister to God's will and pleasure. No matter how many spoken prayers we may send up to Heaven, we still have not attained a state of true inwardness until all the requirements are fulfilled. These include the most thorough possible cleansing of the heart, a life of true attrition and renunciation, and the total surrender of all self-love and attachment to personal opinion or to the ego itself.

Based as it is on attrition and true faith and arising out of our love for God, constant prayer at its most intense is an endless, all-embracing fusion of our will with His, an increased desire that His will be done. True inwardness in its most intense form is a state in which the soul is perpetually "tuned in" to the love of God. This in-flow and out-flow of divine love also permeates our work and blesses it. We no longer do our work for our own satisfaction, for other people's admiration, for gain, but simply for God's holy pleasure, for His interest and honor. We share the life of God, His will, and His love.

In this spirit of love we shoulder our daily cross. We perceive God's hand and providence and, without resistance, joyfully accept it. We submit patiently, delighted to be permitted to do His holy will.

This submission in turn opens our eyes more fully to the many small joys that blossom on the way. It gives us an intensified awareness of the beauties of nature, of order, and of grace; of satisfaction through study, the employment of our talents, and intercourse with our fellow men. We get more enjoyment from beautiful flowers, from the flight of birds, and from other spectacles of nature. All the good things that nature and culture offer for our delight are appreciated with deeper intensity. We see behind all these things the infinite abundance of God and His boundless fatherly goodwill, ascribing every good thing that comes to us to His bounty. Nor do we stop when we have reached this point. The impulse of gratitude itself lifts our whole being into harmony with God; it becomes a prayer.

(d) Automatically, too, many spoken prayers and pious deeds arise from this attitude. They are the flames that spark up out of the perpetual glow, that feed this glow, keeping it alive. Now we begin to "pray without ceasing" and "from a grateful heart praise God in hymns and psalms." Now we begin to understand what the Apostle meant when he said: "Redeeming the time. . . . Become not unwise, but understand what is the will of God. . . . Be ye filled with the Holy Spirit [the Spirit of love], singing and making melody in your hearts to the Lord; giving thanks always for all things, in the name of our Lord, Jesus Christ, to God the Father" (Eph 5: 16–20).

A life of true inwardness can develop only out of a life of true attrition, and it expresses itself in unforced prayer, not merely in studied, memorized, spoken prayers, but in the attitude of soul, the desire for perpetual unity with God that springs straight from the heart and is completely drained of self. This desire automatically finds utterance in words without artifice, without studied form. Such spontaneous prayers are like flames that start up from the intense glow of abiding love. The labors, commotions, annoyances, temptations, and difficulties of everyday life are only incentives, food, as it were, for prayer. They direct our attention to God, materializing as prayers of gratitude, petition, or simply involuntary exclamations of love. Then we truly "live God" in all things all the time.

2. HOW INWARDNESS AND ACTIVITY CAN BE COMBINED

The greatest mistake we can make is to regard inwardness and activity as being mutually antagonistic. On this mistaken premise we try to arrange a compromise: prayer for inwardness, work for the active impulse. But they must not have anything to do with one another! Pious exercises are pushed into a corner of the day's potential, completely cut off from the rest of life's affairs. They are supposed to have influence on the soul only during the time allotted to them for that purpose. Prayer is likewise locked away in little drawers and compartments, only to be taken out for airing at certain times or as convenience permits. Thus, prayer becomes a short, transitory act, a momentary flight of pious aspiration, but not a powerful life-principle giving the soul a definite link-up and direction. It does not impregnate our thought or direct our actions. It is something quite unessential to our lives. Where this conception exists, there can never be a true union of inwardness and activity.

A second mistake: In our daily activities, often unconsciously, we do not primarily seek God and God's pleasure. Although we may not be willing to admit it, we do put ourselves first, seeking our own advantage, gain, honor, success, credit, and importance among men. We are forever trying to serve two masters. We are perpetually trying to do two things at once—to serve ourselves and at the same time save our souls. We act from the human standpoint and not truly from the standpoint of God, glorifying Him and directing all things to His will and pleasure. All too often we halt before the human standpoint even in the care of souls and in education, without penetrating to God's intention and the actual purpose of our existence. The personal viewpoint—in the last analysis, selfishness—kills true inwardness just as it really kills all righteous activity.

A third mistake: We limit true inwardness—"prayer without ceasing" (i.e., intercourse with God)—to attention, reason, and imagination, instead of making it a spirit that will take possession of our willpower, sweeping our soul and our whole being along with it. Inwardness is not only, and certainly not essentially, "thinking of God" or a convulsive effort to conjure up in our mind visions of God. It is a state of mind and will; it is love of God, a continuous urge to loving adoration. It is active love of God in the sense of works conforming to God's will and of unforced, voluntary acts of prayers. We pray to God in just the proportion that we love God. Our inwardness extends as far as, and is as intense as, our love of God is sincere. We prove that by the sincerity with which we are willing to work and to suffer for His sake.

How can we combine inwardness and activity?—By overcoming these three faults and eliminating them from our minds and our lives. This is the first step.

We can go a step farther and turn our daily life into a prayer: first by starting the day with Mass and the customary prayers and reflections and by interrupting our tasks from time to time for the prescribed religious practices; then by putting all that we have to do on a prayerful footing. Our attitude of prayer influences our activity if we bring our whole will to bear upon it. Thanks to this attitude we can exclude as much as possible from our lives anything that would be displeasing to God, even the smallest disloyalty or conscious imperfection, whether by intention, motive, or thought. Thanks to this attitude we can resolve to do everything in our power to perform our duties conscientiously, in conformity with the rules and directions and with complete submission of our own wish and will. Thanks to this attitude we can do our work faithfully and endure with utter resignation whatever unpleasantness, difficulty, annoyance, or suffering it may involve, accepting patiently the trials of the place in life to which He has assigned us.

This attitude of completely merging our will with God's is the state of constant prayer to which we aspire; it makes of our lives one perpetual *Gloria Patri*, a loving "Hallowed be Thy name." We pray all the time, because we see God in everything, and we unify our life with His. From this attitude opportunities will arise, quite of their own accord, to renew our acts of praise and gratitude; to express our joy in God's nearness, in our complete surrender to His will, offering up our love as a sacrifice and an act of adoration to Him. In this way we shall "pray without ceasing."

★   ★   ★

DOES THIS seem impossible or too difficult?

Of course, "prayer without ceasing," true inwardness, is not an undertaking we can treat lightly, taking it up "on the side," as it were. It is not accomplished by reciting a lot of stock prayers and spending hours on our knees. If these are to serve true inwardness, they call for an attitude of soul that is possible only where hindrances that oppose prayer are swept aside ruthlessly and often with painful, relentless effort. The soul must attain a high degree of purity and freedom before the true spirit of prayer can take up permanent habitation there.

How far have *I* gone toward the attainment of this goal?

17. *The Mass*

PART I

I will go up to the altar of God.
PSALMS 42: 4

THE IDEA OF THE EUCHARISTIC SACRIFICE

The focal point of pious Christian life is the Sacrifice of the Mass. There is no greater privilege for Christians than that of assisting at the Eucharistic Sacrifice, which was instituted by the High Priest Christ and which He permits His servants in the Church evermore to renew (Encyclical *Mediator Dei*, Nov. 20, 1947). Therefore, it is of the highest importance that Catholics should fully understand the divine sacrifice in which they are permitted to take part.

There was a time when few outside the clerical profession could interpret the Mass in liturgical terms. It became the custom to explain all the ceremonies and details of the sacrifice allegorically: that is, each ceremony of Mass was looked upon as the representation of some historical episode in the life and Passion of our Lord. This "allegorical" interpretation became a folk custom (closely linked with the Passion Play) and lasted right through the centuries, from the ninth to the sixteenth.

From then on this interpretation gave place to theological-dogmatic considerations: the celebration of Mass was then preferably looked upon as an act of adoration, a thank-offering by the Church or, rather, by the congregation assisting in the celebration. The struggle of the Church against Protestantism brought with it, after the Council of Trent (1545-63), added emphasis to the sacrificial aspect of Christ's death and underlined the character of the Eucharistic Sacrifice as a sacrifice of atonement. Only very gradually were all these different interpretations coordinated, and the greatest strides in this direction have been accomplished by the liturgical revival of the present century, a most noteworthy contribution being the encyclical of Pope Pius XII—*Mediator Dei*.

(a) What does the celebration of Mass mean? What is its object? Its aim is to give us an opportunity of identifying ourselves with the act of surrender, adoration, and exaltation to the Holy Trinity that Christ our Lord demonstrated by the whole of His earthly life and particularly by His death on the cross. In this offering of Himself for the sins of the world, Christ performed the greatest sacrifice, the only perfect sacrifice the world has ever known. He takes us with Him into this sacrifice of adoration and surrender to God so that with Him and through Him we may offer to God the perfect exaltation of which only He is capable. It is an offering of homage that leaves far behind any we could make of our own efforts. An inestimable grace has been conferred upon us in granting us access to the celebration of Mass.

In one sense Mass is offered in memory of our Lord, to fulfill the injunction Jesus laid on His apostles at the Last Supper: "This is my body, which is given for you; this do for a commemoration of me" (Lk 22: 19).

The celebration of Holy Eucharist is a memorial to our Lord's Passion and death. "For as often as you shall eat this bread and drink the chalice, you shall show the death of the Lord, until he come" (1 Cor 11: 26). Its theme is the Passion of Christ. The Church, by means of the Eucharistic celebration, keeps our attention constantly fixed upon this. Thus, every time we go to Mass, we are led again to the foot of the cross on which our Savior suffered and gave His life for us personally—for each and every one of us.

In the celebration of Mass we assist in the reconstruction of all that the Son of God made man suffered inwardly and outwardly, in His soul and in His body, on the Mount of Olives, before the High Priests, before Pilate, at the pillar, at the crowning with thorns, and on the way to Calvary, before He was finally nailed to the cross and left hanging there between two thieves. We recognize in His sufferings and death the triumphant expression of His loving submission to the Father, of His willing obedience. "He [became] obedient unto death, even to the death of the cross" (Phil 2: 8). We recognize in this the proof of His inexpressible love, since he made this sacrifice for each one of us, to atone for our sins. He did this for us in order that we might become children of God and share with Him the Father's love. He "loved me, and delivered himself for me" (Gal 2: 20). "Having loved his own . . . he loved them unto the end" (Jn 13: 1) and gave them the highest proof of His love by offering up His life as "ransom" for their sins (Mk 10: 45).

We recognize in the Mass all that He suffered in expiation of our sins, atoning in our stead and reconciling us with God. By His sacrifice He gained for us not only God's forgiveness for our sins but also our admission to joint sonship with Him as children of God. We owe our salvation to the death of Christ on the cross. By His sacrifice He opened Heaven for us and made us coheirs to all the riches of the Father. In the Eucharistic celebration we recognize Christ's own homage, adoration, and glorification of the Holy Trinity: for Christ alone can extol God to His complete satisfaction, and in the Mass our adoration is absorbed in His, being thus rendered acceptable to God. For only "through Him [Christ] and with Him and in Him is all honor and glory to Thee, Almighty Father, for ever and ever" (Canon of the Mass).

In the liturgy the memory of Christ's Passion and death is

closely linked with His Resurrection and Ascension, just as together in His life on earth they formed one continuous chain of events. Nevertheless, the Eucharistic celebration underlines Christ's death, for the symbols of the sacrament, the bread and wine, do in fact represent the body and blood of our Lord (see *Mediator Dei*).

Holy Mass is at the same time a commemoration of the Last Supper. Here we take part in the reenactment of the Lord's Supper (1 Cor 11: 20). We eat the bread and drink the cup in which we "show the Lord's death" (1 Cor 11: 26); but before we do we must examine ourselves, for "he that eateth and drinketh unworthily eateth and drinketh judgment [punishment] to himself, [in] not discerning the Body of the Lord" [from ordinary profane food] (1 Cor 11: 29). It represents the blessed bread and wine our Lord shared with His disciples in His last meal on earth, and so it recalls vividly the circumstances leading up to His death. It is the divinely instituted meal in which the faithful renew and strengthen their bond of relation with God every time they approach the communion rail.

But the Eucharistic celebration at the altar is even more than this. It is a sacrifice—the offering of a sacrifice, the sacrifice our Lord instituted at His Last Supper in Jerusalem. He gave it to the Church with the injunction: "Do this in commemoration of me" (Mk 14: 22–24; 1 Cor 11: 24–25). The bread we eat in Holy Communion is the body of Christ offered up for us; the wine we drink is His blood in which "the New Testament" was founded (1 Cor 11: 25).

The Council of Trent, in dealing with the erroneous teaching of the Protestant revolt, stresses especially the sacrificial character of the Mass celebration: "Christ the Lord, eternal Priest in the manner of Melchisedech, wished to bequeath to His beloved bride, the Church, a visible offering. Therein His death on the cross was to be represented, preserving His memory to the end of time, and giving us healing power to be used for the forgiveness of sins which are daily committed. He brought His body and His blood to the Father in the form of bread and wine" (22nd sess., ch. 1). The Blessed Sacrament on the altar is not a simple memorial to the Passion and death of Christ but a true and actual sacrifice, in which He, the divine High Priest, by His bloodless offering, repeats what He did on the cross. He represents the offering of His body in the outward symbols of bread and wine. "His death, which actually did happen, is reenacted every time the sacrifice of Holy Eucharist is offered on the altar in the symbols that clearly represent Jesus Christ" (*Mediator Dei*).

(b) The celebration of the Eucharistic Sacrifice is the reenactment of the sacrifice that Christ the Lord made on the cross. In the bloodless offering he repeats that sacrifice. He gives Himself to the Father as a wholly acceptable offering. The Mass, therefore, might be described as the self-sacrifice of Christ. He, the Lord, is the offering that is brought to God in the celebration. Only this one sacrifice and no other is completely satisfying to God. On the altar, Christ consecrates to the Father His life, His blood, His heart and everything it embraces of homage, love, praise, virtue, merit, and the power of petition for grace and pardon. He takes up in His sacrifice everything he prayed for, performed, and suffered during His life, from the first moment, from Nazareth, through His ministry, to His last moments on the cross: "a pure, spotless sacrifice well pleasing to God."

He is at the same time the High Priest who offers up the sacrifice: "the same priest who at that time offered Himself on the cross" (Council of Trent). We look to the altar where the High Priest Jesus with pure heart and pure hands celebrates the sacrifice. The human priest is only the instrument. Through him Christ, the actual priest, officiates at the altar. He is present in the consecrated bread and wine and offers Himself to the Father—albeit bloodlessly, not in the gruesome manner of crucifixion. In the two species, bread and wine, "whereby the condition of His death is represented" (Herder, n. 69), He offers to the Father the same loving submission He offered on the cross.

Therein lies the great triumph of the Eucharistic celebration; it is the same sacrifice that Christ made on the cross, and it denotes the same homage to the Father—adoration, glorification, thanksgiving, ransom for sins, petition. Hence the value of the Mass: it is Christ offering Himself up in boundless love for God and for us. It embraces glorification, praise, thanksgiving, and atonement, all in the one and only manner completely satisfying to God. By taking part in the celebration we can satisfy our own longing to honor, praise, and glorify the Father, by offering ourselves to Him in Christ. "Through Him, in Him, and with Him, all honor and glory to Thee, O God" (Canon of the Mass).

The sacrifice of the Mass is also the offering of the Church. It is not Christ alone who offers the sacrifice. He celebrates the sacrifice as Head of the Church, in the most intimate living union with the Church. Around Christ, participating in the sacrifice, are gathered all the members of the Church, on earth, in Heaven, and in Purgatory. In the person of the celebrant the Church offers up the Body and Blood of Christ, the sacrifice. "We, Thy servants [priests] and Thy blessed people [the Church], offer up in the sight of Thy Majesty a pure, holy, spotless offering" (Prayer after Consecration). "Most closely linked with the High Priest [Christ], together with Him and through Him, we are permitted to offer up this sacrifice and, with it, also to offer ourselves" (*Mediator Dei*). Christ, officiating, offers Himself; we, assisting in the divine celebration, offer ourselves with Him. Thus the Church, in Heaven and on earth, is united with Christ in the sacrifice, and consequently it becomes the Church's sacrifice, and our own.

In the Mass we are drawn into the sacrifice that Christ offered on the cross so that we may be "crucified with Him." The object of the Mass is to impress upon our soul the mystery of the cross, according to the Apostle: "I am crucified with Christ. I live, now not I, but Christ liveth in me" (Gal 2: 20). "So we, too, become offerings for the greater glory of the Father. . . . We should attach ourselves in the closest possible way to the High Priest. Together with Him we should offer up the sacrifice and at the same time offer up ourselves" (*Mediator Dei*).

What the Eucharistic Sacrifice really means is that we and the Church should offer ourselves with the crucified Christ in the Mass—in one common sacrifice, actuated by one united will. But we can accomplish this only insofar as we enter completely into the sacrifice of our crucified Lord, bowing to the commandment of God, emptying our soul of all self and filling it with the spirit of sacrifice, obedience, humility, surrender, with Christ's strength to love and to adore and His hatred of all that is sinful—filling it with His spirit of penitence and atonement. Only in this way will we succeed in offering to the Holy Trinity the tribute due to its exalted majesty and thus share in the blessing of salvation.

Our part in the celebration of Mass depends entirely upon the extent to which we identify ourselves with the sacrifice and allow ourselves to be offered with Christ. The deciding question is whether we can enter into the spirit of the sacrifice on the altar. Participating in Mass means more than following the text—observing the ritual with pious attention. There is far more to it than the stirring drama of the liturgy, the choir, and organ music.

To be offered up in an equally mysterious and actual inner death, like unto that which we commemorate in the consecration of the sacrificial elements of bread and wine. . . . The bread and wine are consecrated and cease to be what they were before. They die and at the same time become something else, something quite new: the body and blood of Christ. Something analogous must happen in ourselves when we assist in the celebration of Mass. We must look upon ourselves as bread and wine. The mortal man with all his human limitations must die in us; we must put on the new man. This is the sacrifice we should desire—we must desire—to bring to God. Our whole being must be unified with the spirit of sacrifice and the loving surrender of Christ Himself in the consecrated elements upon the altar.

★ ★ ★

WE THANK God that we have a "pure, holy, spotless sacrifice." We thank God that we are able to offer Him this inestimably exalted offering daily—the Body and Blood of Christ, the very heart of Jesus with all that it contains of adoration and the spirit of obedience, of love toward the Father and mankind, of merit and atonement and powerful petition. In this sacrifice we are able to offer the Father all the adoration, homage, and glorification that are His due.

We constantly remind ourselves that it is essential for us to offer ourselves with Christ and to enter ever more intently into the spirit of atonement, identifying ourselves with the loving, self-sacrificing surrender of Christ on the cross and in the Sacrament on the altar.

We leave the divine celebration in the consciousness of having been offered up, brought to God with Christ. With renewed readiness for sacrifice, we enter upon our tasks and duties, demonstrating in our practical affairs and in our intercourse with others the strength we have received to endure, to be patient, to work, to suffer, and to love our neighbors as a result of participating in Mass. We carry its influence into our working life with a cheerful and obedient assent to whatever labors or trials God may send us throughout the day.

18. *The Mass*

PART 2

If thou didst know the Gift of God.
JOHN 4: 10

HOW WE RESPOND TO THE EUCHARISTIC SACRIFICE

IF THE Mass is Christ's sacrifice, the sacrifice of the Church, and our own sacrifice, then it becomes a matter of the highest importance to know how we should assist at its celebration. Everything in our Christian life and prayer depends upon our participation in the Eucharistic Sacrifice, for the celebration of Mass is the peak of Christian piety. It is the form of adoration most pleasing to God; it is the highest form of praise and thanksgiving, of petition and atonement to God for our sins. It is the source, in Holy Communion, of all divine grace. Therefore a great deal depends on the proper approach to Mass.

Many do not know what to make of the Mass and pass the time in some devotion or other or in reciting certain prayers arbitrarily chosen. Some people fill in the gaps with contemplation. Some priests read their breviary. And so it goes. They do not realize that as baptized Christians they are bound to enter fully into this sacrifice, which, by permitting them to share in its blessings, provides the kernel of faith that anchors them to a life of prayer and piety. They do not realize that by participating in the Mass they exercise their right to "royal priesthood"—actually the primary purpose of life—to which Baptism gives them full title.

We owe the greatest debt to the liturgical revival for having set as its chief goal the propagating of knowledge regarding the Eucharistic Sacrifice. "The height and to some extent the central point of Christian religion is the mystery of the Holy Eucharist, instituted by the High Priest Christ, which He permits His servants in the Church evermore to renew" (Herder, n. 65).

Consequently, nothing can be more important for Christians than to know the right way of participating in the Mass. But we can do this only by identifying ourselves with the self-sacrificing spirit of Christ Himself in the crucifixion. We come to Mass because of Christ and in order to offer ourselves with Him to the Father: to be "at one and the same time an offering with Him" (Herder, n. 101). Therefore, it is absolutely necessary that we should be linked with the High Priest as closely as possible and that we should do our utmost to reproduce in ourselves the condition of being filled with the same spirit of sacrifice that our Lord brought to the cross.

We come to Mass in order to be offered up with the crucified Christ to the Father, so that we "likewise become one with the sacrifice of Christ" (Herder, n. 101). For this it is necessary that we should be bound with the closest ties to the High Priest and, as far as this is possible in our mortal state, "enter completely into the spirit that filled our Redeemer's soul when He made His sacrifice on the cross" (Herder, n. 80). How can we enter into this condition, filling our soul with the self-sacrificing spirit of Christ?—By outwardly and inwardly surrendering ourselves completely to the ritual in progress at the altar.

Our exterior participation may take various forms. It is a good thing to follow the text in a missal, joining in the prayers and chants; or we can participate actively in a communal or sung Mass. But there are no essential rules for outward participation. As we actually come to Mass in order to assist at the sacrifice and to be offered ourselves, the sacrifice is necessarily and primarily an interior experience, and we must adjust our exterior behavior to the best of our ability.

The most important thing is the inner attitude with which we approach the sacrifice. This consists of "uniting our soul as closely as possible with our divine Savior; that He may daily fill our life with increasing holiness, enabling us to offer more and more homage to the Father" (*Mediator Dei*).

This deep interior participation in the sacrifice of the Mass depends to a large extent upon the attentiveness with which the text is followed and the intelligence brought to bear upon the symbols and ceremonies, distinguishing particular details for different feasts and commemorations that fall on various days of the Church calendar. It also depends on the readiness with which we permit the spirit of the numerous prayers, epistles, and gospels to sink into our souls. Conscious understanding of these is certainly good and desirable—but by no means essential to worthy participation in the Holy Mass.

The right attitude is essentially a matter of the line we deliberately take in directing our will: that is, the way we approach the sacrifice by merging our own ego more and more in the sacrificial spirit. It depends upon the earnest effort we bring to bear upon reproducing in ourselves, as we stand with Christ before the cross, the actual spirit that filled Him as He offered Himself to the Father, thus bringing to life in our own soul the underlying principle of the sacrifice. Looked at in this way, worthy participation in Holy Mass means a constant preparation for the part we have to play in the celebration—the ceaseless labor of a lifetime. It embraces the whole of our daily life with all its labors, struggles, sacrifices, and difficulties.

The actual interior reaction, however, must be revitalized every time we attend the celebration. Excellent aid is afforded by the preliminary service of prayer preceding Mass. The prayers in common use, which reach their climax in the

Confiteor, are also excellent for putting one into the right frame of mind. The nine repetitions of the *Kyrie Eleison* help to lift our spirit. Whoever approaches the altar of sacrifice must also shake off the dust that has again settled on his soul since the last celebration; he must come in a calm, collected state, filled with contrition, repentance, and the will to atone. He must be inwardly and outwardly reconciled to, and at peace with, his neighbor. "If thou offer thy gift at the altar, and there thou remember that thy brother hath anything against thee, leave there thy offering before the altar, and go first to be reconciled to thy brother, and then coming thou shalt offer thy gift" (Mt 5: 12–24).

Another useful custom for stimulating the spirit of sacrifice is practiced extensively on the Continent. In this the congregation reenacts what the early Christians did when they passed in procession before the altar, bearing their gifts of bread, wine, money, and other offerings as a token of their willingness to make sacrifice. We join in spirit this impulse to give when we add our contributions to the collection, along with our hearts, our self-will, our contrition, atonement, and longing to surrender our whole life to God and live henceforth for Him alone, accepting humbly whatever trials He chooses to send us. This attitude vividly realizes the self-surrender that is the very heart of the sacrifice. Members of religious orders may in such a procession renew the sacred vows they made on profession, each time bringing an increased ardor, a deeper desire for complete union with Christ, to the joint sacrifice being offered on the altar. Any offering placed on the paten is silently and prayerfully linked with the great sacrifice in which we join with the priest.

The Preface enables us to associate ourselves with the choir of angels adoring and singing praises, in the *Sanctus* thrice repeated. Then we join with the community of souls and saints in Heaven and approach the sacred moment of the Elevation in a united spirit of sacrifice and self-surrender. Just as the heavens opened for Solomon and flames descended to consume the sacrificial offering, so now Heaven opens for our offering of bread and wine. A sacred fire descends, accepts the sacrifice, and carries it transformed to the presence of God. This fire from Heaven is Christ, the Lord, our High Priest and sacrifice in one.

When the words of Christ spoken by the priest at the moment of Transubstantiation are fulfilled, Christ in person from that moment is present in the Blessed Sacrament on the altar. In laying it upon the altar, the priest offers the bloodless sacrifice to God the Father. We join with the priest in bringing Christ, our sacrifice, to God; the sacrifice Christ offered up on the cross and that is, in fact, Himself—His Sacred Heart, with all its love, its submission, its adoration, reverence, thanksgiving, merit, and atonement; with all the power it possesses for petition, for pardon, for the procurement of grace. Christ the Lord takes up in this, His sacrifice on the cross, everything that He has surrendered to the Father from His first moment on earth—all that He has prayed, worked, endured, and suffered, in Bethlehem, in Nazareth, on the road to Calvary, on the cross. "Remembering the salutary sufferings, the resurrection, and the glorious ascension of Thy Son, our Lord Jesus Christ, we bring to the sight of Thy Majesty a pure offering, a holy offering, a spotless offering, the holy bread of eternal life and the chalice of eternal healing"—that is to say, Christ the Lord, on the holy altar in the form of the surrender that He completed on the cross and now offers as High Priest and sacrifice.

We bring this sacrifice to the Father as our offering, our very own, to make up that which is wanting in our inadequate prayers; as our thank-offerings, as ransom for our sins, as our adoration and glorification of God. In this act we doubly confirm the assent of our will.

We give our assent in the first place to that which is proceeding in the mystery on the altar: Christ offering Himself as He did on the cross. A joyful acceptance of all that He in

His Sacred Heart offered by way of love, prayer, gratitude, atonement for our sins, and intercession on our behalf and on behalf of our loved ones. We give our assent to the fact that He humbled Himself, becoming obedient unto death, even the death of the cross, to release us from sin and procure our admission to a share in His glory. We give our grateful assent to the boon conferred upon us in being able to offer to God His Sacred Heart, with all its goodness and holiness, as a substitute for our own unworthiness. "All praise to Him that cometh in the name of the Lord. Hosannah in the highest!"

In the second place we give the assent of our will to the offering of ourselves with Christ in the sacrifice. We desire in this sacred moment to be lifted up out of the earthly and temporal; we desire to be brought quite close to God, to surrender ourselves to Him, to live solely for Him and no longer for ourselves, for our own spirit and our own will—in unity with the sacrificial surrender of our Lord and Savior on the cross. What we offer to God in the bloodless sacrifice of the Eucharistic celebration must, however, be followed through in the flesh-and-blood reality of our daily life, in an earnest and sincere assent to Christ's words: "If any man will come after me, let him deny himself, and take up his cross, and follow me" (Mt 16: 24).

Anyone who wishes to participate worthily in the Eucharistic celebration must be quite clear on one point: this approach we have been describing goes far deeper than the mere entertaining of elevated thoughts, understanding the theological implications, or appreciating and enjoying the liturgical forms. Assisting at Mass is a very serious matter. It goes to the very heart of Christian existence: to our mysterious but actual interior union with the crucified Christ. It means that we must, this very day, with complete self-abandon, choose the way of the cross, determined to shoulder with utter resignation the efforts, bitternesses, trials, and sufferings the present and the future may bring us, in the

spirit of humility and all-embracing obedience that charac-
terized Christ Jesus. "He [became] obedient unto death,
even to the death of the cross." Sacrificing ourselves with
Christ, we also may say: "My meat is to do the will of Him
that sent me" (Jn 4: 34). Then, truly, "I live, now not I, but
Christ liveth in me." We incorporate this assent into the
Our Father, throwing into it all our desire for union with
the spirit, the will, and the heart of the Lord, who at this
very moment is praying it with us and with the whole of our
fellow worshippers in the community of the Church, in
Heaven and on earth.

The degree of our actual response to the inner meaning of
the Eucharistic Sacrifice depends upon how fully we are
willing to identify ourselves with our Savior, joining with
Him in His obedience and submission to the Father. It is all a
question of assent: the attitude of will we decide upon in the
sacrament of Holy Communion. Communion and the
sacrifice are really indivisible; whoever makes the offering
ought to take part in the divine repast—that is, receive Holy
Communion.

Through Holy Communion Christ, the sacrifice, enters
personally into our soul. He fills and impregnates it with His
spirit of sacrifice and His willingness to be sacrificed, His
complete surrender to the Father. This gives us strength to
meet the hard reality of everyday life; to conduct ourselves as
people who have offered themselves with the crucified
Christ to God. It makes our sacrifice in good earnest one
that is pleasing to God. The words of the deacon or the celebrant—"*Ite, missa est*"—do not mean merely "Go now; you
are dismissed." They are really an assignment, a call to go
forth into the rough and tumble of the world and continue
there, in utter submission, the sacrifice we have just assisted
in, lifting all that we may be called upon to bear and do as a
further oblation to God, a further assent to His holy will and
commandments.

Our Savior, who with such unfathomable love sacrificed

Himself on the cross for our sake, desires above all things to flood our souls with His strength and spirit of love, so that we may, at the communion rail, strengthen the ties that bind us in a living community of our brothers and sisters in the Church. We are to be "one body and one soul." Hence, every time we receive Holy Communion we are called anew to the compassionate, long-suffering, forgiving, helpful, service-rendering power of love—that quality the Apostle has in mind when he writes: "[Love] is patient and is kind; [love] envieth not, . . . is not puffed up; seeketh not her own; is not provoked to anger, thinketh no evil; beareth all things, believeth all things, hopeth all things, endureth all things" (1 Cor 18: 4–7). It is a call to that love of which the Lord says: "This is my commandment: that you love one another, as I have loved you. . . . I have chosen . . . that you should bring forth fruit" (Jn 15: 12, 16)—the fruit of selfless, ministering, helpful Christian love. In the strength of His love, which He gives us in Holy Communion, we can fulfill the task before us.

Holy Communion also serves to unite us more closely day by day with the crucified Savior offered up in the Mass. "Let this mind be in you, which was also in Christ Jesus: Who, being in the form of God, . . . [took] the form of a servant, being made in the likeness of men. He humbled Himself, becoming obedient unto death, even to the death of the cross" (Phil 2: 5–8). As Pope Pius XII explains, "These words of the Apostle demand of Christians that they shall, as far as is humanly possible, reproduce in their souls the spirit with which the soul of the Savior was filled. With obedient submission, with adoration for the Majesty of God, with homage, praise, and thanksgiving. They are also required in a certain measure to adopt a condition of sacrifice; to deny themselves, submitting voluntarily and gladly to penance, shunning all sin, and making atonement. The final requirement is that we shall all, with Christ, take to ourselves the mystical death of the cross, so that we may apply to ourselves

the words of St. Paul: 'With Christ I am nailed to the cross' "
(*Mediator Dei*).

It will be seen therefore that the reception of Holy Communion lies on a line running parallel to that of the celebration of Mass that contains or precedes it. Both go to the very
root of being a Christian, because we are linked with Christ
in His death (Rom 6: 8). A Christianity that does not offer
up this sacrifice, drawing ever nearer to the cross in imitation
of Christ crucified, is no true Christianity. What the Lord
says of Himself applies also to Christians: "Amen, amen I say
unto you: unless the grain of wheat falling into the ground
die, itself remaineth alone; but if it die, it bringeth forth
much fruit" (Jn 12: 24). That is the law that governs the life
of Christians. For we are all, since we are "baptized unto
death" (Rom 6: 4), alike "bearing about in our body the
mortification of Jesus, that the life also of Jesus may be made
manifest in our bodies" (2 Cor 4: 10).

The liturgical celebration draws to a close. But its effect
and its purpose go on working in us. What we have assisted
in offering at the altar of sacrifice is imprinted on our active
life and expresses itself in the powerful assent of our will to
everything the day may demand of us; that is to say, we are in
the condition of willingness for sacrifice, which participation in the Mass has produced in us. Therefore the entire day
becomes a thank-offering for the grace we have received in
the sacred sacrifice and a preparation for taking part in the
renewed sacrificial celebration tomorrow: for every time we
take part worthily in the Mass we increase our readiness for
sacrifice and strengthen our will to that end.

Participation in the Eucharistic Sacrifice is the fabric, the
very center of Christian life, transforming it more and more
into that which it essentially should be: union with Christ in
the death on the cross and true discipleship of our Lord. Is it
not an exalted boon—that we should possess the right of
participating in the Holy Mass? How grateful we ought to be
for this!

We cannot begin to estimate the grace conferred upon us in the gift of Christ, the High Priest, and, through Him, priests who have been ordained so that they may offer up the sacrifice in which we are permitted to participate, offering ourselves together with the Savior.

"If thou didst know the gift of God . . ." (Jn 4: 10).

19. *Brotherly Love*

This is my commandment; that you love one another.
JOHN 15: 12

WE LIVE the life of God in Jesus Christ when we are in rapport with Him. Essentially, Christian life is a life of sacrifice to the Father; a life of complete unselfishness and, at the same time, a life of love toward all men, of "brotherly love," love of our neighbor. Christ's attitude toward mankind is one of compassion. His love rises to our need and flows in where it is needed. Christ is the Good Samaritan who cannot pass us by. His love obliges Him to bend over us, pouring oil into our wounds and bringing us into the shelter of His holy Church, where we may be healed and live. "This man receiveth sinners, and eateth with them" (Lk 15: 2). We live in His life. Therefore our life must also be a life of brotherly love. "Thereby they shall know that ye are my disciples, that ye love one another as I have loved you."

I. FORMS OF LOVE

(a) With wise providence God has given us the urge to love and to be loved. Fundamentally, man's love is sensual love. It is born in all mankind. It is the most natural passion that rules in the heart of man: the irresistible attraction to a thing or to another person as soon as we discover in that thing or that person whatever is to our taste, or pleases us, or corresponds with our ideal. Whether we master this passion, making it a lever for good to ourselves and to others, or whether we allow ourselves to be carried away by it to our own destruction and to the ruin of others, depends on ourselves. Passion, the fancy of love, can be the source of immense good to humanity and also the source of almost all evil, according to whether it is guided and guarded or unbridled and unrestricted. This sensual love, this irresistible attraction, exists also in animals. We all know from personal experience how much we must be on our guard against these attractions and inner urges.

(b) There is a pure natural love. We find it among mankind everywhere. It is not so much a feeling as a good intention, an attitude of will, a virtue, a result of work and freedom. It is an expansion of the soul, the annulment of "I" and "thee." It overcomes the narrowness and pettiness of the personal self. The broader and more noble the love, the richer the soul that loves. Love widens and deepens. It deepens our sensitivity and perception and understanding. One can only understand perfectly that which one loves. Love—pure, noble love—opens one's eyes and quickens one's insight. It opens up depths that are imperceptible to those who do not love or are indifferent. As soon as it has reached the state of truth and goodness, love imparts to the soul nobility and perfection, in which at the same time all natural moral perfection and all natural virtue are included.

This pure and noble love is characteristic of all pious, God-fearing people. It must express itself in a high-minded, natural human goodwill toward our neighbor, whoever he may be; as an upright desire to make others happy, to serve, to be helpful; as noble endeavor, justice, good nature, affection, consideration, and politeness. This natural virtue of love means that we are not forever thinking of ourselves or seeking our own advantage. It means that we try to see only good in other people, and even when they have left the path of virtue it does not cease to regard them as fellow creatures who have an indestructible germ of goodness in them. It goes out of its way to find food for hope that they will one day be brought back to the high state from which they have fallen.

The natural virtue of love often springs more or less from

selfishness, because love is a thing that human nature imperatively demands. But where it is based on pure motives it rises to moral heights that should not be underrated. It is actually the normal basis of supernatural Christian love, of peace and the welfare of the family, the community. Hence the maxim of theology: the supernatural does nothing either to set aside or destroy nature but takes it as it is, elevating and ennobling it. So we arrive at nothing less than this: a really pious Christian is also a naturally noble, unselfish, fine man; an admirable character, full of kindness and loyalty, incapable of injustice in speech or action, incapable of lying, or double-dealing, or dishonesty; a character who cannot be otherwise than gracious, kind, and loving to everyone under all circumstances.

Clearly this kind of love calls for effort and self-mastery. Love has to prove itself by self-denial, by endurance, by patience, persuasion, forgiveness, and "turning the blind eye." It must know how to humble itself. True and noble love must be discriminating: it must know what it may love and how much. It loves because it must love. The highest natural love is a matter of willpower, of virtue. But it is still only a natural, not a supernatural, virtue.

(c) Supernatural brotherly love is an altogether higher virtue. It is natural love cleansed of all its imperfections and transformed into love of God and one's neighbor in accordance with the commandment of Christ.

This supernatural quality is based on love of God and is actually the florescence of divine love. It is brotherly love for the sake of mankind, not for the attraction that draws us to one another, but for the sake of God's will. He gave us a commandment: "Thou shalt love thy neighbor as thyself" (Mt 22: 39). This prompts us to love our neighbor because we love God. It prompts us to see in mankind not only the creation of God but God's very image. It makes us recognize our fellow man as a being into whom God has poured His life and His love, as a being He has called to share His life and to live it with Him. This is why we are bound to love humanity. Brotherly love is the confirmation of our belief that God sent His only-begotten Son to save us, and also our fellow man, from the wages of sin. Therefore we must recognize in our fellow man the love with which God surrounds him. We must see in him the divine Father embracing his soul with holy love. We must perceive in the soul of our fellow man God's living and active presence, Father, Son, and Holy Spirit. Therefore, when we love our fellow man with supernatural, brotherly love, that love automatically becomes love of God.

Our Christian brotherly love has its roots in faith, in believing the words of Jesus: "I am the vine; you the branches" (Jn 15: 5); in recognizing man as the limb of Christ, the body. Body and limbs are one. Therefore, Christian brotherly love makes true the words of the Lord: "Amen I say to you: as long as you did it to one of these, my least brethren, you did it to me. . . . Amen I say unto you, as long as ye did it not to one of these the least, neither did you do it to me" (Mt 25: 40, 45). We recognize and love in our neighbor Christ the Lord, the member of the body, the branch of the vine.

Therefore, in essence, brotherly love is nothing less than love of God, of Christ. That is why theologians teach that brotherly love is the same as love of God and Christ. Nothing distinguishes the two virtues or forms of love from one another. They are one and the same love. We love our brother for the sake of God and Christ. We love in our neighbor God and Christ. Because we love God we love him —and all others whom God has called to be His children or who are yet to receive that call. Therefore, our Christian brotherly love embraces all mankind. We see God, Christ, in all, something divine, something belonging to God, something that needs to be treated as holy and venerable. This love unites us all, among ourselves and in unity with God. It makes us all one with the body of Christ. Hence Christian brotherly love towers high above all natural human love. It is God-love, Christ-love. We love God and Christ precisely to the extent that we love our neighbor.

Christian brotherly love expresses itself in practical terms as a holy, supernatural reverence and esteem of our fellow man as a child of God in whom the Father is well-pleased (Mt 3: 17). In honoring our neighbors we honor Christ, since they are members of His body. We honor in our neighbor the tabernacle inhabited by the Holy Spirit; we honor in him the chalice into which God has poured His life. Brotherly love expresses itself in a desire for justice and truth in thought, word, and deed, in judgment, in speech, and in behavior toward our fellow man. It expresses itself in an inclination always to see what is best in others, to overlook their failings; in a spirit of patience, long-suffering, and forgiveness, in a readiness to respond to every need, material and spiritual. It expresses itself in a desire never willingly to offend another person, be it in behavior, word, or thought, judgment, or repulsion. It expresses itself in a genuine readiness to show love wherever we can or should; in a willingness to live peacefully, one heart and one soul with the rest of the holy family of God, children of the one Father, members of the divine body of Christ, all filled with the spirit of Christ, the spirit of unity and love.

Supernatural love is strong enough even to love its enemies. "Love your enemies. Do good to them that hate you. . . . And to him that striketh thee on the one cheek, offer also the other. And him that taketh away from thee thy cloak, forbid not to take thy coat also. Give to every one that asketh thee, and of him that taketh away thy goods, ask them not again. . . . Be ye merciful, as your Father is also merciful. Judge not, and you shall not be judged. Condemn not, and you shall not be condemned. Forgive, and you shall be forgiven. Give, and it shall be given unto you, good measure and pressed down and shaken together and running over shall they give into your bosom. For with the same measure that you mete, withal it shall be measured to you again" (Lk 6: 27–38).

2. THE MEANING OF BROTHERLY LOVE

"If I speak with the tongues of men and of angels, and have not love [charity], I am become as sounding brass or a tinkling cymbal. And though I should have prophecy and should know all mysteries . . . and if I should have all faith, so that I could remove mountains, and have not love, I am nothing. And if I should distribute all my goods to feed the poor, it profiteth me nothing. . . . There remain faith, hope, and love, these three: and the greatest of these is love" (1 Cor 13: 1–3, 13).

Where love is lacking everything is lacking. Where love reigns there is no lack, for love embraces everything that is needed for perfection.

(a) Christian brotherly love is the measuring rod of our unity with God. On Holy Thursday, when our Lord instituted the Holy Eucharist just before His Passion commenced, He prayed His high-priestly prayer. His greatest anxiety was that we should be "all one." "[I pray] that they all may be one, as thou, Father, in me, and I in thee; that they also may be one in us; that the world may believe that thou hast sent me" (Jn 17: 21). Father, Son and Holy Ghost, the Trinity in Unity . . . one nature, one action, one creation in the unity of love, the Father united with the Son in the Holy Spirit. Here is the archetype and pattern of all community life. "That all may be one, as thou, Father, in me, and I in thee." We are, therefore, vitally linked with God. We live the holy, blissful, inner life of God exactly to the extent that we love one another.

So that there shall not be the slightest mistake about this, our Lord prays further: "And the glory which thou hast given me, I have given to them, that they may be one, as we also are one" (Jn 17: 22). The Father gave His Son the glory of sonship, the glory of a child of God, and this same glory the Son of God passed on to mankind, since, through sanctifying grace in Baptism, He made us coheirs with Him. Why did He do this? "That they may be as we are."

Sanctifying grace unites the hearts and minds of Christians just as the divine nature of the Father is united with the Son in the Holy Spirit. For sanctifying grace means participation in divine nature, divine life. We live the life of God; we benefit by sanctifying grace and confirm our sonship only by loving one another, by bringing our will to bear on the cementing of unity—one heart, one soul, in communion with Christ in God. Sanctifying grace, because it is the channel of God's life, is the unifying force that establishes unity in heart and soul. The first fruit of sanctifying grace and divine sonship is therefore an urge to brotherly love in all its forms. Love is born of God. "And everyone that loveth is born of God and knoweth God . . . for God is love" (1 Jn 4: 7–8). We love God only as much as we love our neighbor. Food for thought. . . .

(b) Brotherly love is the measuring rod of our unity in spirit and intention with Christ. His intention toward us is one of divine love. "How have I loved you!" How He has loved us. In the mystery of His being made man? In redeeming us on the cross? All this in spite of our sins, in spite of our unworthiness, although He clearly foresaw how little we should requite His love and show our gratitude; how often we should repay Him with disloyalty, prefer crazy notions and all kinds of false gods to Him, offending Him and crucifying Him again and again.

How He loves us in His Eucharistic life in the tabernacle of the altar! Everything breathes love, a love that thinks only of our welfare and consumes itself in goodwill, prayer, and sacrifice. His life, His love, His strength are continually flooding our soul. He is forever quickening us inwardly with His support, His inner and outer influence through the happenings, the surprises, that overtake us, and all the lessons we may draw from them, if only we will accept them as such. His one purpose is to purify our soul so that it may more completely unify itself with Him and with God, thus rendering us rich, holy, and happy. How much His love has in store for us in eternity! "Eye hath not seen nor ear heard, nor hath it entered into the heart of man, what things God hath prepared for them that love him" (1 Cor 2: 9).

So much does He love us. How much have we in common with Him in spirit and intention? Just as much as we possess the faculty to love. "This is my commandment, that you love one another, as I have loved you." We do not, therefore, fully live the life of Christ until we have succeeded in loving our neighbor.

(c) Christian brotherly love is the measuring rod of our love of Christ. Our Savior leaves no doubt in our mind about this. He will eventually judge us by this standard. What will be the deciding factor?—Love, brotherly love. According to what law? The law: "As long as you did it to one of these, my least brethren, you did it to me. . . . For I was hungry and you gave me to eat; I was thirsty, and you gave me to drink; I was a stranger and you took me in. Come, ye blessed of my Father, possess you the kingdom prepared for you from the foundation of the world" (Mt 25: 34–40). In brotherly love we love Christ, of whose body we are members, the vine of which we are branches. Christian brotherly love is love of Christ.

Many people ask themselves whether they love Christ. They look for signs whereby they can ascertain whether they love Him. The unmistakable sign is brotherly love. Whatever we do to injure our neighbor—even if only in being cold toward him, unjust or indifferent, critical in our thoughts and judgments, words and deeds—is a sin against Christ, against a limb of Christ, for whose sake Christ was made man and died on the cross, to save and sanctify his soul. It just cannot be reconciled—the desire to love Christ at the same time with unloving behavior toward one's neighbor.

(d) Brotherly love is the measuring rod of the standard we set for our inner life, particularly our life of prayer. We say the Our Father, "Give us this day our daily bread. Forgive us our trespasses. Lead us not into temptation. Deliver us from evil." We can honestly ask for all this only if we have actually carried it out by our attitude toward our neighbor. We attend Mass daily. We pray and offer ourselves up as a community, with one another and for one another. If we have enmity in our hearts toward anyone, we close the door, we lock ourselves out, and we fail to enter into the spirit of "we pray, we offer up." Therefore we do not fully participate in the holy sacrifice. We receive Holy Communion, "the sacrifice of unity, the bond of love" (St. Augustine). The first function of Holy Communion is "communion in the Mystical Body of Christ," unity of heart, "that they may be all one." The fruit of Holy Communion is essentially love, the will to be at peace with one's neighbor, the endeavor to fall in with our fellow man in heart and soul, despite all the difficulties love is bound to encounter from our own selfishness and ego-worship.

So many approach the altar in the morning and receive Holy Communion; yet no sooner do they return to everyday life than they begin to pile crime upon crime against the law of love, in thought and speech, in judgment and in behavior. Despite Holy Communion, despite prayers and meditations, they criticize and speak unlovingly, they are moody, depressed, cold toward others, complaining, impatient, unyielding. Is that true love? Where are all the good intentions, the tolerance, the kindness, the goodwill that love demands? It is not as though, even with complete guard on one's behavior, one can entirely escape error! But such errors are quickly repented and made good. A strong, clear resolve to forgive, to be forbearing, helpful, sincere in a desire to serve, rules the soul. This resolve spurs one on to action, to deeds. Where this will to love, this eagerness to yield, is firmly rooted in the soul, unmistakable proof is at hand that our

Communions, our confessions, our meditations, and our prayers are well in order. They are genuine and fruitful.

(e) Brotherly love is the standard by which we can calculate the extent of self-love in ourselves. Self-love has a trick of disguising itself as virtue, self-denial, ardor, energy. But we have a standard by which we can measure exactly how much we are under the domination of self-love and how it affects our practical dealings with our neighbor. Self-love is highly sensitive, envious, suspicious, cold, prone to partisanship, injustice. True brotherly love means the death of self-will, personal preferences, wishes, and attractions. Whoever earnestly wishes to practice brotherly love must possess the virtues of humility, patience, and unselfishness. Only great virtue can love in truly Christian fashion. For love "is patient and is kind; [love] envieth not, . . . is not puffed up, . . . is not ambitious, seeketh not her own; is not provoked to anger, thinketh no evil; rejoiceth not in iniquity, but rejoiceth with the truth; beareth all things, believeth all things, hopeth all things." Love embraces virtue and perfection. Where love is strong, it overcomes self-love.

★   ★   ★

"THIS IS my commandment; that ye love one another, even as I have loved you." The very heart of Christian life is love, supernatural, brotherly love. It is one and the same love as that of God for Christ. All the commandments are based on love, and all commandments are fulfilled through love. Genuine love demands more than a passive tolerance toward our neighbor. It expresses itself in active good works, in constructive thoughts and words. It does not rest upon its laurels but is forever seeking new ways to express itself.

Let us examine ourselves carefully on the subject of love—not only to discover any respect in which we have failed, but to ask ourselves honestly whether there is anything more we could do to make others happy, to love our fellow man "as He loved us" and still loves us.

"Wonder not, brethren, if the world hate you. We know that we have passed from death to life [i.e., that we have sanctifying grace, which makes us children of God] because we love the brethren. He that loveth not abideth in death [in sin]. Whosoever hateth his brother is a murderer. And you know that no murderer hath eternal life abiding in himself. In this we have known the charity, because He hath laid down His life for us; and we ought to lay down our lives for the brethren. He that hath the substance of this world, and shall see his brother in need, and shall shut up his heart from him, how doth the charity of God abide in him? My little children, let us not love in word, nor in tongue, but in deed and in truth" (1 Jn 3: 13–18).

20. *Unity with Christ*

> *I am the vine; you are the branches.*
> JOHN 15: 5

GOD IS the fullness of life. His life flows from the Father to the Son and pours from the Father and the Son into the Holy Spirit. For love of us God decided to let us share His life, that we might possess it and live it with Him. But before the stream of divine life pours over us, it is caught up and held in "the firstborn among many brethren" (Rom 8: 29). "Because it hath well pleased the Father that in him all fullness should dwell" (Col 1: 19). What Christ received He desires to pass on to us. Therefore God appointed Him the head of the body, the Church (Col 1: 18). "I am the vine; you are the branches." Vine and branches are one complete organism; they live and work together and together bear fruit. So are we, the baptized, united in Christ, the vine, in one body, through which flows the life He possesses in all its fullness.

What is the most important practical requirement of Christian life?—That we should dwell in Christ, and He in us . . . that we should be grafted on to Him in one living organism, with His life flowing through us. "As the branch cannot bear fruit unless it abide in the vine; no more can ye, except ye abide in me. If a man abide not in me, he is cast forth as a branch that is withered, and men gather them and cast them into the fire and they are burned."

The essential part of Christian life consists of our being *in Christ*, identified with Him in living unity, members of Christ. We talk so much about this, that, and the other form of prayer; we argue about different kinds of piety; we differentiate between so many different "movements" that we scarcely notice how often we are skating around the unimportant circumference instead of drawing ever closer to the heart of the matter, the actual truth and center of our Christian faith. Let us get back to essentials, to the pivot of our faith, to that which makes us Christian—the "being in Christ" so often alluded to by St. Paul.

1. "in christ jesus"

If we read the Epistles of St. Paul properly, two important points emerge: What Jesus does, He does not do alone—we do it with Him; and again, what we do, individually, we do not do alone—Christ does all these things with us. Christ is one with us. "For if we be dead with him we shall live also with him" (2 Tim 2: 11). "We are buried with him" (Rom 6: 4). "We are risen with him" (Eph 2: 6), and "through him we have access to the Father" (Eph 2: 18). On the other hand, Christ lives in those who are His—as the life of the vine lives in the branches (Jn 15: 5). He lives in the needy, in the sick, in the beggar who asks for a piece of bread (Mt 25: 35). He is persecuted in us; He suffers, fights, and conquers in us, "filling up" in our sufferings, "those things that are wanting" (Col 1: 24).

We are linked with Christ historically. We are linked with the historical figure, Jesus Christ, who was born in Bethlehem; who lived in seclusion for thirty years; who then emerged as a Heaven-sent Master and Teacher, preaching in Galilee and Jerusalem, healing the sick, working miracles; and, after He had fulfilled on the cross the task of redeeming mankind, who rose on the third day from the dead.

We are linked with Him, the infallible Teacher of truth. We long for truth. Who gave it to us?—Christ, and Christ alone. He alone has "the words of eternal life" (Jn 6: 68), "full of grace and truth" (Jn 1: 14). In the confusion of opinions and views, of religions and confessions, of daily altering crosscurrents of thought, we alone possess the truth, all truth (Jn 16: 13) in Christ, in our unity with Christ.

We are linked with Him as the shining example for our inner life and our life in the world. "I am the way" (Jn 14: 6). We are called "to be conformed to the image of his Son" (Rom 8: 29). "I have given you an example, that as I have done to you, do you also" (Jn 13: 15). "Learn of me" (Mt 11: 29). "Born, crucified, dead, buried, risen from the dead, and ascended into Heaven." With these words the Credo shows us Christ's way and also our way, with its milestones, its twists and turns, its ascents and its declines. We must "suffer with him, that we may be also glorified with him" (Rom 8: 17). We follow the example of His virtue, His holiness. We reflect upon His self-chosen debasement from the crib to the cross, His love of poverty, His utter submission to the will of the Father, His life of voluntary suffering; the striking example He gave us on the Mount of Olives, before Annas and Caiphas, at the judgment before Pilate, at the release of Barabbas, at the pillar, amid the cruel mockery of the Roman Guard, and in the last dreadful hours before the crucifixion. "[He] who, being in the form of God, . . . [took upon] himself the form of a servant, . . . he humbled himself, becoming obedient unto death, even to the death of the cross" (Phil 2: 6–8). He is the ideal of morality and holiness and the realization and fulfillment of that ideal. He is that for each individual person and for all mankind, for all races. How fortunate are we that we have such an example and that we can model ourself upon it!

We are linked with Him as the Redeemer who has secured for us remission of sin and reconciled us to God, transforming us from children of wrath to children of the all-loving Father. What should we do without His redeeming love, His act of redemption? How could we have a moment's true happiness or inner joy? But for Him, where should we find a single star of hope to light the way to salvation for our soul and body? "Being justified therefore by faith, let us have peace with God, through our Lord Jesus Christ, by whom also we have access through faith into this

grace wherein we stand, and glory in the hope of the glory
of the sons of God. And not only so, but we glory also in
tribulations, knowing that tribulation worketh patience; and
patience, trial [experience]; and trial, hope. And hope con-
foundeth not" (Rom 5: 1–5). We are redeemed in Christ
Jesus and only in Him. "In none other is our welfare."

We are linked with our dear Lord Jesus in His throne on
the right hand of the Father. We are linked with Him in the
same mysterious, inner, living union, perpetually, without
pause or interruption.

The living Christ lives and works among us in His holy
Church. The Church is not a mere abstraction, but a tan-
gible reality, the outward manifestation of the unseen presence of our Lord. Uninterruptedly through the centuries,
since our Lord's time on earth, He has gone on living and
working in His Church. "Jesus Christ, yesterday, today, and
the same forever" (Heb 13: 8): on and on, everywhere, the
Church, growing and fulfilling herself. The Church is His
body. In the Church He lives and accomplishes the work of
grace for the healing of mankind—and only in His Church.
We are only linked with Him, and we only share in His grace
and redemption by entering into the life of the Church. We
hear the voice of Christ in the Church; in the Pope, in the
bishops, and in the God-ordained clerical administrators.
"He that heareth you, heareth me; and he that despiseth you,
despiseth me; and he that despiseth me, despiseth him that
sent me" (Lk 10: 16).

He lives with us in the sacraments. In the sacraments we
recognize the Good Samaritan who pours oil (Baptism) and
wine (Holy Eucharist) into our wounds and heals them.
Christ, the Lord, "He it is that baptizeth" (Jn 1: 33). He
speaks the words of forgiveness in the sacrament of Penance
through the mouth of the priest. "I loose thee from thy
sins." He lives with us and continues in us His work of salvation. In the Church we make contact with His spirit and His
strength.

He lives with us in the Holy Eucharist. In the Mass He daily comes into our midst, so that we may offer up the great Sacrifice with Him to the Father . . . His heart, His love, His adoration, His atonement. He embraces us in Himself and takes us up in His offering, so that our adoration, our surrender to God, our thanksgiving may be worthy of the eternal God and glorify Him. We are united with Christ in the holy Sacrifice! And in Holy Communion He enters deep into our soul, that His inclinations may become our inclinations; His thoughts may be our thoughts; He with us, we with Him; one heart, one soul in a living exchange, one spirit in loving unity—an exchange that is inexpressible in natural human terms. He envelopes our soul with His holy soul and floods it with His life. He overpowers and transforms it, so that it lives only by His life. He draws the soul up into His purity and His spirit. The soul is conscious of this. "I live, now not I, but Christ liveth in me."

He lives in us as the vine lives in and through its branches (Jn 15: 5). "As the head in relation to the limbs, as the vine in relation to the branches, so Christ stands in relation to those in a state of sanctified grace, taking up their good deeds, fulfilling and perfecting them, so that they may be pleasing and meritorious in the sight of God" (Council of Trent, 6th sess., ch. 16).

This, our living union with Christ, is illustrated in the Mass. At the offertory the priest pours water into the chalice. The water combines with the wine and is lost in it, the mixture becoming one substance; and in the Elevation it is consecrated the Blood of Christ. "I am the vine, you are the branches." Here we have the very heart of the union with Christ in Christian life. Christ is the truth we obey. He is the way, the pattern on which we model ourselves. But that is not the whole Christ. It is not sufficient that we should know the Christ who once dwelt on earth and who died for us on the cross. It is not enough that we should realize His virtues, His doings when He lived. Christ did not only say:

"I am the truth and the way." He also said: "I am the life." "I am come that they may have life, and may have it more abundantly" (Jn 10: 10). We are permitted to live the life that is in Christ with Him, exactly as the branch lives the life of the vine and the body the life of the head. As the body, as the vine, He lives His holy life in us through the sanctifying grace He exercises in us and the attendant graces with which He is continuously flooding our soul from His inexhaustible font of life and love.

It is the Savior's wish to share His life with us. It is our part to let the divine life have its way in us. The actual mystery of Christian life is that Christ lives in every one of us. He is the truth for that purpose; He is the way to that end. We hear His word and try to model ourselves upon Him, so that He may live on in us. He not only secured grace for us by His death on the cross, as the risen Christ He continues to shower graces upon us in proportion to our need and our readiness to receive it. His spirit nourishes us, as the sap of the vine nourishes the branches.

"I am the vine; you are the branches." Living, organic unity in Christ. . . . It is the Savior's intention that our life, our thought, our endeavor, our activities, and our sufferings should be directly linked up with His life, carried, fed, and nourished by His life; that He, the Son of God made man, should determine our thoughts, lead our will, set our strength in motion, hold all the strings of our life in His hand, so much so that our life would be simply a radiation from, a repetition of, His life within us, just as the life of the branches is a radiation from, a repetition of, the vine's.

2. OUR NOBILITY

We are members of Christ, branches of the vine. "O man, recognize thy nobility!" (St. Leo). The nobility of the baptized, the Christian. . . . We are not just human beings with natural gifts and tasks. We are incomparably more than that.

We are members of Christ. From the state of sin and eternal damnation in Hell we have been lifted into the state of grace and life in order that we may be children of God, coheirs with Christ.

Members of Christ! The most essential and important thing in life, also the most difficult, is to make our heart swell with this consciousness. "Learn holy pride," St. Jerome admonishes the Virgin of Eustochium. Righteous, well-founded consciousness of nobility in Christ sits well on Christians. "I am a limb of Christ." Recognize your nobility, your greatness, Christians! Learn to grasp who you are, what you are! Learn to wonder, to be astonished, learn to swell your heart in your blissful faith and in the consciousness of being a member of Christ!

Recognize in yourself a green, life-laden, fruit-bearing branch of Christ, the Tree of Life, whose roots reach deep into the earth and whose branches touch highest Heaven! Recognize in yourself a limb, a branch of Christ, the body, the vine, living, grafted-on and ingrowing, nourished by His strength and grace. "And of his fullness we all have received, and grace for grace" (Jn 1: 16). Why should you fear? "Not that we are sufficient of ourselves to think anything as of ourselves; but our sufficiency is of God" (2 Cor 3: 5). True, we are but dust, sinful, miserable, weak. But we are members of Christ, alive with His life, His strength coursing through our veins, His grace illuminating us. "I can do all things in him who strengtheneth me" (Phil 4: 13). I am stronger than all passion, stronger than all the lures of the world and the lusts of the flesh; in my veins pulses the strength of the all-conquering Christ! Know your strength in Christ! Believe in it! Lean upon it!

Limb of Christ. . . . Therein lies your strength and greatness. You are organically one with Christ, the body, the head. Therefore, the life that flows from Him through you may determine and guide you, if you will but let it have its way, if you do not isolate yourself, cutting off the flow of divine strength by proud self-reliance, regarding your own natural strength and intellect as sufficient for your needs. By making your will Christ's will—by allowing the head to guide the limb—by merging your every wish and endeavor in the desire and purpose of Christ, you will achieve an inner harmony productive not only of peace but also of results.

Limb of Christ. . . . Recognize your brothers and sisters also as limbs of Christ. Have a holy, supernatural reverence for your brother and your sister and remember, "As long as you did it to one of these my least brethren, you did it to me" (Mt 25: 40). Should we not regard our fellow man with much more reverence—think of him, speak of him, more gently and kindly—if we looked upon him as a limb of Christ?

(a) Because we are members of Christ we carry within us the spirit of Christ. Christ, the head, is filled with the Holy Spirit, with grace, with the light, the strength, the glow of the Holy Spirit. Filled with this, His spirit, he radiates the same spirit through the limbs. "In this we know that we abide in him, and he in us: because he hath given us of his spirit" (1 Jn 4: 13).

Christ's spirit lives in us. It directs our mind to God, to all that is true and good. It gives us resolution to carry out the principles of Christ and the gospel in our lives, to avoid sin, and to keep God's commandments. It makes us strong in self-control, in self-denial, in sacrifice, and in willingness to bear the cross with Christ. It impels us to love God, to love Christ and our neighbors. It is the spirit of true wisdom, of understanding of divine truths, of counsels, of strength, of piety, of the holy fear of God. It makes us love solitude, prayer, poverty, chastity, self-denial, meekness, and obedience.

Christ's spirit in us. . . . It reminds us, prompts us, warns us, speaks to us; He is ever at hand to help us with His illumination and grace. We are never alone, never thrown back on our own feeble human resources or efforts in our union with

Christ. How much time we waste thinking of our incapacity, our unwisdom, our insufficiency, the dangers that threaten us, the obstacles that stand in our way! His spirit works in us. How strong we are, how immensely capable of every mighty and holy effort in our union with Christ! His spirit lives in us and is not idle. "He, to whose will and might all things are subject, protects and stimulates us against our own madness and unwisdom, density of intellect and hardness of heart" (St. Thomas Aquinas, *Summa Theol.*, I–II, q. 68 a, 2 ad 3). And we? We agitate the surface but fail to dive into the depths, where the spirit of Christ, the Holy Spirit, has its habitation and works in the Holy of Holies within our soul.

(b) Grafted to Christ, we have His life flowing through us just as the life of the vine flows through the branches. This life, which the only-begotten Son of God received from the Father, which flows from Him forever, and which we, also, have in us through Him, is incalculably higher in every respect than the natural life of the senses of human intellect and understanding. In the act of being made man our Savior carried the stream of divine life, which issues from the Father, into the human nature He received from the Virgin Mary. In the Holy Eucharist this life flows from the head, Christ, to the body (the Church) and to the limbs (ourselves). "And of his fullness we all have received" (Jn 1: 16).

We share the possession of this divine life with Christ, the head. This priceless possession is worth more than all the wealth of the universe put together—more than gold or goods, more than knowledge and achievement, more than honors and power, more than talent and health and all human greatness. We share this possession with Christ.

We not only share the life of Christ, the head, we also share His submission to the Father's will, His zeal for the well-being of our neighbor, His prayers, His works, His sufferings. When we suffer, Christ, the head, suffers in us, the limbs. "The Church suffered in Christ," writes St. Augustine, "as He suffers for the Church when she suffers." Christ suffered, fought, and vanquished in the martyrs. When we pray, Christ, the head, prays with us, and we pray with Him. For, as St. Augustine says, "Head and limbs are one flesh, so that what the one is, the other is, and the two cannot be separated."

When we are gathered together in the spirit of prayer, withdrawn within ourselves, then the Lord is in our midst, continuing to live in us the life He led when He fasted for forty days, the life He led in His nights of prayer, and that He leads among us incessantly in the Blessed Sacrament. When we labor, our painful efforts unite with the toil and blood and sweat of our Lord, and take on the value, the beneficence, the fruitfulness of Christ's share. Our life of obedience identifies itself with that of Jesus, who was obedient unto death, even the death of the cross, and who still shows the same obedience in the tabernacle. Our life of poverty is the same as that of Jesus in Bethlehem, in Nazareth, on the cross. "The son of man hath not where to lay his head" (Mt 8: 20). It is our great privilege that our life merges into the life of the Head whose limbs we are and that we share His life, being permitted to live it with Him and continue it, on and on to eternity.

We also share the life of Christ in its outward aspect, for how can the limbs go any other way than that to which the head leads them? "We suffer with him, that we may be also glorified with him" (Rom 8: 17). "Ought not Christ to have suffered these things and so to enter into his glory?" (Lk 24: 26). "If they have persecuted me, they will also persecute you" (Jn 15: 20). Our union with Christ necessarily entails a bond of suffering and death with Christ here on earth. That is the meaning of the crosses and the sufferings we encounter on our earthly pilgrimage.

We share the life of the Head when we participate in the Mass. We are drawn into His exalted adoration and glorification of the Father. "Grant that the sacrifice we offer through him, in him, and with him in thy sight may be pleasing to thee, O God." We are with Him in the offering to the Father, one Host with the great Host of Christ. We cross out our own personality and yield ourselves completely to be possessed of God's will and providence. Host to Host in actual life!

(c) In-grown into the life of Christ, we share all that He has: His body, His blood, His heart, His merits, His suffering—everything is given to *me*. I of myself am nothing. Where my prayers, my deeds, my sufferings are feeble and inadequate, He places His at my disposal, so that I may offer them as amplification for what is wanting in my own. Everything that He has, we share. "The sufferings of Christ are given to all who are baptized, just as if they themselves had suffered and died. That is why everyone who has been baptized may be freed from sin, as if he had himself atoned for them" (St. Thomas Aquinas, *Summa Theol.*, III, q. 69, a. 2).

We share all that He has: His truth, His grace, His saints, Mary, His mother, His apostles and martyrs, His confessors and virgins, their merits—all their prayers, their atonements, their sufferings, their virtues, their labors—and the sufferings of all the Church Militant on earth.

We are joint heirs with the Head in His glorious heritage. There He will "reform the body of our lowness, made like to the body of his glory, according to the operation whereby also he is able to subdue all things unto himself" (Phil 3: 21).

United with Christ, we are "the elect of God, holy and beloved" (Col 3: 12). Beloved . . . God sees in us the limbs of his only-begotten Son, "in whom he is well pleased" (Mt 3: 17). "He that hath not spared his own Son, but delivered him up for us all" (Rom 8: 32). His heart, His love. . . . Our life may lie in ruins about us; everything may be taken from us; life may be hard and bitter. Yet the comforting gleam of faith gives us the assurance: I am beloved, divinely, truly, loyally, and deeply loved; I am the object of God's goodwill and care; lovingly He watches over me. What have I to fear? "If God be for us [and he is], who is against us?" (Rom 8: 31).

We are vitally linked with Christ, all-holiness; a part of Him, sharing His freedom from sin, His purity; as pleasing to God as the head to which we belong. "Shall we continue in sin, that grace may abound? God forbid! For we that are dead to sin, how shall we live any longer therein?" (Rom 6: 1–2). "Shall I then take the members of Christ and make them the members of a harlot? God forbid!" (1 Cor 6: 15). No, as members or limbs of Christ, organically one with Him, we can, correctly speaking, be nothing less than holy. Dead to sin, we can only "live God," incapable of breaking His commandments, opposing His will. We can only live the pure, holy life of Christ, in Him, through Him, and with Him. To be holy and to become saints is not the exclusive prerogative of members of religious orders. It is within reach of all Christians in every walk of life.

If only we were more conscious of this! We are too little aware of being living parts of Christ, as in-grown into His life as the branch is to the vine. Hence all our weakness: our own futile efforts, our wrestling and battling seem so much more important! The power of evil is so very near that it can easily fill us with terror, then trip us up. We can see only wickedness around us. The saving grace, our unity with Christ, seems so far away. Why cannot our heart swell with St. Paul's certainty of victory, or with the strength of the holy martyrs?

Let us believe more in our unity with the living Christ! "I am the vine; you are the branches." Let us make the "in Christ Jesus" of St. Paul a living reality in our lives. Here lies our nobility, our strength, our wealth. We are copartners with Christ in His divine life.

21. *The Holy Will of God*

Thy will be done.

TO LIVE God's life, to will God's will. . . . Complete identification of our will with God's, in purpose, in motive, in manner, in reason. . . . God's will is divinely beneficent and wise. We, too, are holy and wise when we give God complete possession of our will and let His will be done in us. We live the life of Christ, the head, to the extent that we do just this. Christ knew no other will than the Father's. "My meat is to do the will of him that sent me" (Jn 4: 34). In conformity to the will of God He humbled Himself, "becoming obedient unto death, even to the death of the cross" (Phil 2: 8). "Not everyone that saith to me, Lord, Lord, shall enter into Heaven, but he that doth the will of my Father who is in Heaven" (Mt 7: 21).

The goal is clearly defined: it is the sharing of God's life forever, in all its perfection, in Heaven. "Thy kingdom come." That is the way we are heading when we cheerfully, completely, relinquish our will to God's. For all practical purposes this sums up the whole task of acquiring Christian perfection. The love of Christ and God is bound up with the uniformity of our will and God's will. Actually, unity with the life of God is nothing more nor less than yielding our will to God's. Our progress toward perfection lies in "Thy will be done."

God makes His will known to us in two ways: in His commandments, prohibitions, recommendations, and advice; and in the ordinances of His providence, the "acts of God" and the various happenings that determine the course of our lives. The first of these two classes we call the "revealed will of God," while the second comes under the heading of "God's will and pleasure."

I. THE REVEALED WILL OF GOD

(a) This can apply to all mankind, to particular classes of people, or to individuals. It indicates clearly what God wishes and expects of us. This will of God makes itself known in the requirements of nature, in natural intelligence, in reason, in duties to natural morality, in natural justice to our neighbors and to the community, in the requirements of natural good behavior and politeness. It would be perverted piety if we imagined we could ignore the requirements of sound reason. God wishes us to use our reason and give proper consideration to all that we do. He wishes us to use natural means to ascertain His will; He wishes us to confer with others, to use our own intelligence. He has given us our intellect so that we can apply His will to the details of our life. Often we have only our own intelligence to guide us in our decisions.

He makes His wishes in regard to the divine order of things known to us through the commandments of God, through the commandments of the Church, and through the duties of our rank and station in life.

The commandments of God reveal the will of God most clearly. They are the first and most fundamental rules of conduct and also of holiness. It is our first duty to obey them. The more faithfully we follow them, the more we bend our will to God's. The commandments of the Church are the second set of rules that determine our duty and regulate our spiritual life. They are laws of faith for our spirit, laws of morality for our will, and laws of discipline to guide us in what we should do and what we should not do. Unless piety conforms in every respect to the laws of the Church in faith, morality, and discipline, it is self-condemned.

Duties of rank and station determine more particularly

what God requires of us in accordance with our position in life. They are the expression of God's will. We can never attain holiness unless we carry out with all sincerity the duties of rank and station. There is no piety where duties of station are neglected or calls of charity ignored. Duties of priests are embraced in the rules regulating clerical life, and in the liturgical direction and Church laws, where they concern clerics. Those of the religious orders are laid down in their own rules, even down to those that seem of little importance— matters affecting house regulations or orders of the day. Every time the convent bell rings it is the voice of God letting the convent community know what He requires of them. The duties of rank and station for lay Christians are determined by the requirements of the calling they follow. In one way or another we all have some call we must obey, whether we be officials, learned professionals, heads of organizations, workers, parents, teachers, or servants. In the orders, duties, or necessities of his calling, every man may know what is God's will for him personally.

Apart from the commandments (that is to say, apart from acts specifically ordered or strictly forbidden, which, in the strictest sense, must fulfill God's behest and cannot be treated otherwise without sin), there are many other things that God recommends, advises, or suggests. To defy these wishes of God would not be exactly sinful; but we know that in falling in with these wishes and suggestions we give God pleasure. Outside strict commandments and duties God does not demand this and that, but we can please Him by doing more than we are compelled to do. These acts come under the heading of "things that are pleasing to God" and earn us compensating grace.

Where it is a question of attaining perfection we must advance beyond the commandments. Perfection aims at total good. The soul does all the good that lies within its power. It does not ask: "Am I obliged to do this? Is it a sin if I leave it undone?" It goes beyond mere duty to superlative performance within the limits of rank and station. In this frame of mind the aspirant to perfection prays more than he is obliged to; does not confine his attendance at Mass to Sundays and holy days. He goes to confession and Communion not just once a year, as he is bound to do under pain of mortal sin. Love impels him to do more than mere obligation demands. The will of God expresses itself in the impulse that leaps at every opportunity to do good deeds. The more loyally we obey these impulses the more we serve God and grow in grace.

We are also made aware of God's will and pleasure in the promptings of grace within us, provided such inspirations are clear and unmistakable; but it is safest, in this case, to submit oneself to the advice of one's spiritual director. God can, by special favor, make His wishes known to us in these occasional flashes of insight. We do wrong, however, if we disguise some secret wish of our own under such "inspirations," making the pretense of pleasing God an excuse for self-indulgence. If we wish to be perfect, we must obey every impulse God sends us to do good, every clear suggestion we receive from our indwelling grace. It is in these acts over and above duty that the aspirant to perfection differentiates himself from one who is less ambitious and only seeks to abide by the letter of the commandments.

(b) Our duty toward the expressed will of God:

The first thing is to see and acknowledge it—not merely to rest upon the strict performance of one's duty; not merely to obey the commandments of God, the duties the Church imposes upon us, the orders of our superiors, or the laws of the State. We should recognize in all duties, directions, obligations, even in the demands of nature (such as the need for food and rest), and in our social responsibilities of all kinds, the will of God, of Christ, and a means of ministering to God's pleasure. But this presupposes a deep faith. If we think as the majority of people do, we will never attain this high goal. We have to fix the eye of faith clearly on God, on our

Savior. We have to see Him in all our duties and obligations. "Thou desirest this of me. Be it so!" That is the first and perhaps the most difficult step: the prompting of faith, the yielding to faith. "This is Thy will. Thou callest me. Thy will in all, above all," must come to us so readily that it excludes all else on each and every occasion. In order to recognize God's will, we may be guided by the Gospels, the Missal, the rules of our order.

The second thing is to love God's will. Everything depends on love. We must really love the orders, commandments, duties, and rules imposed upon us because we see God, His will, and His good pleasure in all of them. In our natural state, commandments do not sit easily upon us; mankind leans to ease, and duties are a burden. But the will of God, seen under the rough exterior of commandments and duties, lends them attraction. God's laws are for the most part irksome to nature, because they run counter to our own wishes and desires. But if we truly love the will and pleasure of God, then the yoke becomes sweet and the burden light. If we submit to commandments, rules, and regulations unwillingly, they crush us down. If we unresistingly embrace the duty, command, or prohibition in the same spirit with which Jesus at the cross embraced the will of the Father, then we are carried up by the duty itself and united with the Father's loving will.

Loving, consciously cooperating with the will of God, which we see disguised in the order or duty, we are given the strength faithfully to carry out whatever is required of us, down to the smallest detail. This strength gives us power to meet all our obligations. It makes us brave and free. We no longer cling to anything but God's will. We are exact, conscientious, trustworthy, but without pharisaical pride, without pettiness and pedantry, without fear or anxiety. We are not so much concerned with the letter of the law, but in all our duties keep God's will before us and regulate our conduct accordingly. And so, even while concentrating our whole attention on what we have to do, we experience no inner strain. "I have run the way of thy commandments, when thou didst enlarge my heart" (Ps 119: 32).

The third thing is to do the will of God gladly. We must do it with all our might, with loyalty and joy, with complete surrender to the task. We must do as He wishes because He wishes it. In our everyday life we yield our will to God's will, and our activities become an unbroken prayer. This is what we mean by a life of piety, of holiness, of unity with God.

2. GOD'S WILL AND PLEASURE

The will and pleasure of God is not directed to mankind in general, as the commandments are. Neither does it exactly define what God expects of us. The will and pleasure of God is a matter of discretion for each individual personally. This is not a question of what God demands of us but of what we feel impelled to do for Him, each according to the way his own spirit moves him. We place our hand lovingly into the hand of the Father and follow wherever He leads us. When we follow the will and pleasure of God, He bears us up in the arms of providence. We no longer move forward with our own feeble short steps but, with God's arms supporting us, we move with the mighty strides of God, and our progress is rapid.

(a) "All things work together, unto good to such as . . . are called to be saints" (Rom 8: 29). God's providence takes care of each one of us personally. Not even the sparrow "is forgotten of God" and the very hairs of our head "are numbered" (Lk 12: 7). "But a hair of your head shall not perish" (Lk 21: 18).

Behind every chance occurrence of our lives the providence of God may be detected. It orders everything, guides everything, directs everything for our highest individual good, and this applies to all things, without any qualification or limit. It applies to the great world events and their effect on our own small individual lives; it refers to each incident of our working day, even down to the smallest particular. People, whether they wish us well or ill, serve the ends of providence; so do all creatures and things. All are instruments God uses for our advancement and well-being. Nothing happens by accident, even to our inner life.

Providence is at work all the time cleansing our soul, illuminating it, making it fruitful, prompting it to holiness. How tenderly, but at the same time powerfully, it operates! God is forever seizing the right opportunity, the right moment, to subject us to that which is for our highest good. He knows how to adapt Himself to our circumstances and requirements. He alone knows how to set about it and the best means to employ. He alone is wise enough and mighty enough to take into consideration all the factors that influence, or should influence, our life, combining them in such a way that they serve our highest interest by the manner in which they cooperate under His direction.

God's will and pleasure is also to be traced in the dispensations of providence, which for the most part are quite incomprehensible to us. God can do no evil. It is not His will that anyone should do us harm or tell lies about us or treat us unkindly, unjustly. He does not will this, but He lets it happen, although He might just as easily prevent it. The will and pleasure of God makes itself known in everything the day brings forth, inwardly and outwardly, in sorrow, in joy, humiliation, sacrifice, misfortune, difficulties, sufferings, mishaps, injustices through other people, setbacks, unkindnesses, disturbances, annoyances, temptations, illnesses. Nothing happens by chance. "The very hairs of your head are all numbered." Everything we meet with in our lives, one way or the other, is either permitted or positively produced by the will of God, as the just, all-wise, all-loving wish of our eternal Father. "For he hath care of you" (1 Pet 5: 7).

The will and pleasure of God, working in us and for us, is the dominant factor of our interior life. If we are at one with

God's will, we keep pace with God and attain the goal of holiness. Whatever we succeed in doing of our own efforts contributes to our sanctification. But it is always a poor return for the effort expended. We do not get very far that way. Our progress begins only when we start occupying ourselves with God's will and pleasure.

(b) What have we to do in this connection?

First of all, we must perceive and believe. That is the decisive step. We must see God, His providence, His dispensation, in everything. This calls for profound, living faith—a faith that does not rely merely upon the evidence of the senses, nor upon human thought and judgment; a faith that looks to God, to Christ, in all things and regards everything that happens as being God-permitted, God-given. Certainly both joy and grief overtake us here and there through so-called accidents and combinations of circumstances. But our faith looks beyond appearances. It is influenced neither by people nor their opinions. It sees not merely what is unpleasant or hard to bear, the crushing cross, the injustice, the insult, the sickness, failure, disappointment. It looks right through these dispensations to the hand, the loving providence, the holy will of God behind the outward evidence of the senses. We must look beyond appearances to the truth, and there we will find God's will, God's love at work. "Blessed are they that have not seen, and have believed" (Jn 20: 29).

We must enter into the will and pleasure of God with childlike simplicity and blind trust. We must let God work in us through the circumstances, great and small, of our daily life in the world, through the current events that condition our existence. We must have the inner courage to accept whatever God sends in the blind, unreserved confidence that He is working in us and testing us inwardly and outwardly for our highest good. We must accept with gratitude the gifts He showers upon us from His great abundance day by day—the natural and supernatural gifts, the joys of nature with its sun and flowers, the joys of family life, and the pleasures of human companionship, of work, of intercourse with God, with Christ, with Mary and the saints. We must accept, too, the many sufferings and difficulties, the trials of daily life, the patches of interior aridity, the temptations, and all the knocks and unpleasantnesses of outward life. They are nothing but God's will and pleasure in operation, the proof and expression of His love for us, working for our purification, healing, and salvation. We accept the working of God's providence without reserve, without curiosity, without unrest, and without fear, knowing that He desires only what is best for us. We accept all these things with gratitude, feeling His nearness, relying on the help of His grace, and knowing only one answer: "Father, as it pleases thee; thy will be done."

Complete submission to God's providence and dispensation: that is Heaven on earth. On this level the soul finds all dispensations and untoward happenings agreeable, no matter how painful they may be in terms of material man. The soul, arrived at this pitch, loves whatever it may please God to send. Only God's will is of any importance, and identification with God's will is the only thing worth striving for. Such a soul no longer grieves over the loss of a comfort, of a condition, of anything in the world, not even health. It knows that being at one with God demands nothing less than the giving up of all things. In voluntary surrender of all the ties of personality it finds freedom, happiness, Heaven on earth. It knows neither envy nor jealousy, torturing fear, worry, or anxiety. It is emancipated from all these. It is submerged completely in the desire to will God's will. "To love God in the comforts is certainly commendable, if one loves God's will and not the comforts that lie in it. To love God's will in His commandments and counsels [as revealed will of God] is love on a higher plane. But if, for love of God, we can love suffering and tribulation, that is the perfection of holy love; for then we love nothing else, only God's will" (St. Francis de Sales).

★   ★   ★

THE REVEALED will of God—God's will and pleasure; our work—God's work; active piety—passive piety. . . . God's work (the will and pleasure of God) begins to operate in us. We accept it; we follow the inspiration, the inner impulse. So we work hand-in-hand with God, in complete dependence upon Him, allowing His will to do in us and with us whatever it pleases. Out of this marriage of God's will and activity with our own, good deeds are born, great works, deeds for eternal life, and this in greater measure, the more we surrender our will in faith and holy love to the will and workings of God.

Let us examine ourselves on the question: To what extent am I obeying the requirements and the wishes of God? To what extent have I surrendered my will to the providence and the dispensations of God? In my daily, habitual life?

22. On the Heights

God is love.
1 JOHN 4: 8

TO SHARE God's life and live it—this is the purpose for which we were born. But God "is love." His nature, His life, is love. Therefore our life must also be a life of love. We must be caught up in God's love, absorbed in it, carried away by it. Alight with the perpetual glow of divine love. . . . That is the meaning, the goal of our life, for time and eternity.

Happy the soul that can graduate by merit to a life of love! On the heights of love the soul is aware only of God. It lives solely and exclusively for love. Certainly the soul fears sin, but not because it trembles before the justice of God (craven fear); it dreads sin because it loves; and sin hurts, offends, shocks the loving soul so that the fear it feels is innocent and childlike. The soul is completely in tune with God when it loves Him to the exclusion of all else. Love makes it strong enough to give up everything that could be in any way displeasing to God. Love gives the soul power and courage to withstand temptation to disloyalty, selfishness, and resistance; love gives it the strength to make the sacrifices that love demands. Asking nothing but to please God in every way, in its complete surrender the soul is content.

I. DEFINITION OF DIVINE LOVE

Once the soul has attained these heights, can it afford to rest upon its laurels, making no further effort, and enjoying God at leisure? Can the soul dwell upon its own delight in God? Has it outstripped all the sufferings and difficulties that formerly beset its path? Many have believed this and have taught it. But they have been mistaken. It is not so. When the soul has reached the upper regions its real work begins. Now it really needs courage—to sacrifice and to be offered up in sacrifice. What it has suffered before this was a mere prelude, child's play, to what it must suffer now in learning the mysteries of divine love.

(a) Spiritual life on the heights actually involves a radical simplifying of the soul. The more perfect it becomes, the more it resembles God. It loves God for Himself, not for the sake of its own satisfaction. Therefore, everything works in the soul to purify it aims at simplification. As soon as the soul has achieved complete surrender to God, He proceeds to simplify it.

God simplifies the soul in its motives. The loving soul knows only one motive for its love. It loves God for Himself and not for its own satisfaction. It no longer looks to itself or its own interest, but only to Him. Whatever might please Him is the soul's pleasure to do; whatever He wishes becomes the soul's consuming passion.

God simplifies the soul in its method of approach, in the way it sees and judges things. From now on, the soul must learn to see God with the "single eye." It must learn to understand the mystery of Jesus in its wholeness and not, as formerly, piecemeal, in disjointed parts. It must learn to see its neighbor in God, Jesus in its neighbor, living His mysterious life there, as in a limb or branch. In all circumstances and events the soul must recognize the Father at work, shaping everything with His divine wisdom and goodness.

God simplifies the soul in its desires and strivings. From now on it has only one longing, one wish: that God's will be done. It is no longer torn by the thousand and one yearnings, agitations, and anxieties that at one time beset it. The holy will of God is its peace. All its emotions are dissolved in the all-absorbing power of love. It loves what it is permitted to love—its neighbor, its work, prayer, the sacraments; but it loves all these in God. It seeks God's holy will in everything.

God simplifies the soul in its interests. He tears it out of its preoccupation with itself and dissolves all remnants of attachment to its own interests. Then the soul begins to acquire a distaste for all the things that mattered so much in the past—for books, entertainment, art, and all kinds of cultural activities. Now all these things are subordinated to God's wish. Social life becomes burdensome. Good works lose their face value: they are just things through which God expresses Himself, and they belong to Him. Ego retreats into the background. God is everywhere.

God simplifies the whole nature of what should be done or left undone. The soul performs its duty with complete singleness of purpose, careless as to the thoughts and opinions of others. Only God matters. So it goes its way, regardless of all else, if only God be satisfied. No tricks, no artifice, no deception, no double-dealing. Nothing but the fulfillment of His will! Nothing for itself. All for Him. Happy soul. . . .

Another milestone is reached when the soul acquires a new attitude toward prayer. The soul is no longer agitated by the numberless considerations, thoughts, questions, and problems that once assailed it in times of devotion. Prayer becomes quite simple. Half the time it is not even possible to determine what the prayer is about. The soul only knows that it has offered itself up in prayer. It was there, although it might please God to send distractions, involuntary absences of mind, periodical failings of inspiration; still the soul held on, collecting its forces, reassembling stray thoughts, offering itself without struggle, peaceful, happy, always conscious of contact with God. This is the way the soul prays on the heights. It no longer struggles with a mass of details, with this, that, or the other petition. Its prayer has become more calm and silent, full of love-laden trust in God, who knows all its wishes and pours out His love to meet them even before they are spoken. The soul loves.

In professional life the loving soul finds itself similarly

situated. Active labors are carried on not so much for what they are as for Him in whose honor they are performed. Quite unconsciously and automatically, with almost unbroken continuity, the soul is moved to acts of faith, of trust, of love, of gratitude, of surrender. Always there is the underlying desire to give Him pleasure. The soul seeks nothing for itself. Its only wish and desire is to belong totally to Him.

The soul prays without ceasing. Its life is one perpetual intercourse with God. Prayer becomes automatic; it actually forces itself upon the soul. It is now second nature—so much so that most of the time the soul does not even realize that it is praying.

The third milestone marks the so-called passive purification. Until this time, with much self-denial and overcoming, the soul has been able to cleanse itself. The more it climbs the heights of perfection, however, the more God Himself takes the work in hand. He continues and completes the undertaking. His work is incomparably more thorough and penetrating. Divinely competent and drastic, He seizes chisel and mallet, chipping away the last residue of self-love and perversion. He robs the last natural powers—understanding, will, imagination, heart—one after another, of their inborn functions and reduces them to silence. He reaches mercilessly into the very depths of the soul to tear out the last roots of evil, of former sin and shortcoming.

(b) God goes farther. He allows the soul to sink into the lowest depths of its own insufficiency, worthlessness, and insensibility among scruples and despair, to temptations, unchaste inclinations, exasperation, anger, even blasphemy and unlovingness. In this way He shows the soul what it is capable of when left to itself, what could happen if He withheld His grace. With these humiliations and sufferings, troubles on the outside are almost invariably linked; injustices, false accusations, slander, difficulties of environment, and sometimes, too, torturing illnesses, a brimming measure of spritual and bodily sufferings. The soul fears that God has forsaken it. Heaven seems no longer to hear its prayers. It can no longer find the Savior where He was once so close at hand—in the tabernacle, on the cross, in His mysteries. The soul can no longer find its way out of the maze of difficulties and often bitterly reproaches itself about its terrible condition.

But in its lowest depths the soul still clings steadfastly to God. In humble, utter surrender and submission to these trials, its one remaining desire is that God's will be done. The soul makes no complaint of God, only of the tools He employs—the people, conditions, dispensations. It does not desire to change its circumstances. It has surrendered itself to God and is happy that His will should be done in it and through it. In this way God cleanses the soul of its last vestiges of self-love. The purer it becomes, the higher He can lead it toward the summit of love.

On the heights of love . . . a new atmosphere, a new light, a new life on earth. In the lower stages the soul worked through readings, meditations, studies, prayers, various practices, and through human intellect, piling up a certain amount of religious insight. On the heights imagination and understanding often find no more mental images and thought-pictures. It is all simpler, clearer, more spiritual: the holy proximity of God. The world, impressions, experiences of former times, earlier religious revelations—all seem to fall from the soul like an outworn garment. God fills it with a new sort of awareness of His presence. The soul feels that God, whom it loves, takes it more and more into His possession, drawing it into His world. If only it will keep quite still and let Him do His will in it! It sinks into His embrace. Strengthened, transformed, it rises out of itself. Now it is ready for newer, more glorious, more painful, and, at the same time, still more blissful experiences.

2. THE FRUITS OF A LIFE OF LOVE

"By their fruits you shall know them" (Mt 7: 20).

A fundamental law of spiritual life is this: "Every branch in me that beareth not fruit, he [the Father] will take away; and every one that beareth fruit, he will purge it that it may bring forth more fruit" (Jn 15: 2). Still more fruit. . . .

(a) The first fruit of a life of love is Christian innocence. The ways of the world, of selfishness, of semi-piety are winding and artificial. Whoever thinks of himself first, of his own interests, his own honor and glory, his own satisfaction, the fulfillment of his own egotistical plans and intentions, must keep casting sideways glances all around him; he cannot develop the "single eye." What will other people say? How will the matter end?

With the loving soul things are very different. It has surrendered itself to God. It keeps its vision fixed exclusively on the will of God. Its only consideration is the honor of God . . . God only. This disposition makes all craftiness, all dissimilation, all cunning impossible. It eliminates all anxiety as to personal credit, self-interest, or profit. The question "What will other people—my neighbor—say?" is silenced before the majesty of "God only." The one pertinent consideration is: "He wills it so. This is His pleasure." Then the soul has only one more question: "How can I best fulfill His holy will?" No further debate, no hesitation, no caution or fear. Quietly, with complete unconcern, the soul sets about fulfilling God's will. No matter what may happen—let other people think what they please, let the results be successful or unsuccessful—still "God's will, God's will only!"

Innocence of intellect: the intellect bows in awe, adoring the word of God, every word of the Gospels, every wish and every decision of rightly constituted superiors, the Church authorities. It bases no criticism on its own opinions, understanding, or intellectual superiority.

Innocence of heart in relation to God: an innocent, childlike attitude, a complete surrender to the hands of the Father, without disquiet or nervous anxiety. The loving soul implicitly trusts God's love, providence, and guidance; its one care is to do His will entirely, without reserve, without curiosity, without fear; to do His will without fussy questioning and subtle debate.

Innocence toward other people: an upright, heartfelt goodwill. It means an open generosity free from forwardness or disdain; a gentle, patient, compassionate love, which forgets itself to live in peace with others and to do good to all.

Innocence toward oneself: a spirit of patience with oneself and with others; a spirit of order and peace; a spirit free from moods and fancies, from over-anxiety and indifference, from violence and inertia. It fosters an innocent willingness to sacrifice its own will and its own opinions, without calculating the cost of the sacrifice; an innocence that is yielding but not weak, that is willing to give consideration to others, provided this does not mean violating its own principles or neglecting its own duties.

Innocence in one's dealings: no haste or agitation; all innocence that is full of integrity, doing all it has to do with all its might. An innocence that in prayer is concentrated wholly on God, and in its work, wholly on the job in hand, doing what it has to do primarily for God, conscious of His observation, taking Him into partnership, as it were, and seeking His approval always.

Innocence in externals: in dress, in behavior, in speech, in attitude; no affectation, no self-seeking. Everything is for God alone.

(b) The second fruit of a life of love is freedom of heart and spirit. Freedom of heart is something more than an easy-going acceptance of rules, regulations, and established outward customs. Freedom of spirit is the opposite of fear, pettiness, narrowness; it distinguishes between the letter and the spirit, between the means and the end, between common sense and red tape. It is the very reverse of the bigotry well illustrated by the Pharisees, who would "strain out a gnat and swallow a camel" (Mt 23: 24).

Freedom of heart and spirit rests on the words "God only." The loving soul knows that nothing can replace God. It knows that God's gifts are not God Himself. It knows that even when all else is right and good, God is best. It knows that many roads *lead* to perfection, but only God *is* perfection.

Freedom of heart and spirit: the soul at one with God rises superior to unrest, to the irritating and disturbing crosscurrents set up by outward experiences and events. Inwardly it has thrown off its fetters and stands emancipated and disengaged, ready at any moment to leave everything to which mankind, in a state of semi-piety, still clings. He who loves has mastered his lusts, inclinations, and wishes. He is no longer the slave of ambition, avarice, sensuality, ease. He is free and no longer allows worldly considerations to disturb, agitate, or hinder him. Nor does other people's mockery or contempt put him out. He is not insensitive to setbacks, humiliations, insults, but they do not excite or frighten him in any way.

His soul is also fortified against the vicissitudes of his interior life, the ebb and flow of consolations, trials, temptations, and temporary failures that dog its progress to the heights. God only. . . . That is why the soul accepts with utter contentment whatever God may give or take. It never loses its equanimity even when it makes mistakes and the whole misery of failure stares it in the face. No confusion, no discouragement; only humble submission to God's dispensations and unlimited trust in Him.

The soul at one with God does its work without haste or anxiety. It stands inwardly ready in every occupation or duty to leave the work it has grown to love, the position enjoyed, the office worthily occupied, and to sacrifice the promised fruits of seed sown by past labor. Let others reap the harvest. The soul obeys all instructions, observes all the customary procedures, and is loyal in all that it does—but with divine liberty. It does not cling to habits and customs; it does not get excited if some routine detail is passed over; it is ready at all times to drop everything for the sake of its love of greater perfection—everything except the will of God.

The loving soul is not forever preoccupied with questions of health. It does not neglect health, but its attitude is free from worry. It is one of complete calm, ready at all times to bow to the will of God.

(c) The third fruit of a life of love is an incomparable harvest of good. God takes into account the quality, the interior content, of acts of love. The smallest good deed performed from a motive of pure love has more value in the eyes of God and brings the Church more profit than all other works put together. This is the considered opinion of a saintly Doctor of the Church who himself attained the higher pinnacles of love—St. John of the Cross.

Just one act of love. . . . What, then, must be the bliss of those whose whole life is one continuous act of perfect love?

"Everything done from the motive of love is love; that includes labor, exhaustive effort, even death," writes St. Francis de Sales.

The loving soul does everything, whether it be sacrifice, labor, or suffering, out of pure love. Hence all its interior and exterior acts become works of perfect love. Every one of these acts has a value in God's sight that leaves the works of imperfect love immeasurably far behind. Those who love are the ones who honor God completely. They are the wise ones whose deeds have true merit.

The fruitfulness of the loving soul is increased by the fact that its acts of love are not, like those of beginners, intermittent, occurring just now and again. They maintain an almost uninterrupted continuity. Such is the life of the soul on the heights of love. It occupies itself constantly with good works, putting forth all its strength to please God, and these are good works without the slightest trace of self-interest or even human reflection. Each of these deeds puts the soul into a better state for the increase of grace. Each of these deeds gives the soul added strength and impels it to further acts of love. These become habitual and are as easily performed as the drawing of breath.

"The smallest act of pure love has more value in the sight of God and brings the Church more profit than all other acts put together." So what must be the merit of an unbroken succession of these good works performed from the heights of perfect love! What merit for the soul that performs them! For the souls of others! All souls being united, every single soul's condition affects the history and the destiny of all other souls. What therefore can be more helpful to humanity than the loving soul? It is the Savior's effective copartner in the healing of souls, just because its acts are all works of pure love. Thousands upon thousands owe the grace of conversion, of overcoming temptation, of call to the priesthood or a religious vocation, of grace for perseverance, to the silent influence of loving souls.

★   ★   ★

ONLY GOD. . . . Those are the words of the soul on the heights of love. Its life runs its course very near to God, in an atmosphere of Godlike simplicity and complete forgetfulness of self, of perpetual uninterrupted prayer and intercourse with God, a half-painful but at the same time exquisite ecstasy: the mystery of love. Only God . . . hence the life of holy innocence, of enviable inner freedom and independence, of inner peace and divine equanimity; hence the life of unparalleled spiritual, supernatural fecundity, for itself, for others, for the whole Church.

We are all called to the heights of love. That is the goal toward which we are striving. "Thou shalt love the Lord thy God with thy whole heart, and with thy whole soul, and with thy whole mind, and with thy whole strength" (Mk 12: 30). Who is it that completely fulfills this calling?—He of the loving soul, the soul that seeks only God and that knows nothing beyond God.

God only. . . . There is no need to wait until we are old and gray-haired, as if the best years should be given to negative living. While we are still young, from the very start of our surrender to God, we should strive for love and learn to love. Other virtues grow out of love. It is not the best way, to develop love in later years out of the other virtues. On the contrary, we should advance through love to the perfection of all virtues.

"Thou shalt love the Lord thy God with thy whole heart, and with thy whole soul, and with thy whole mind, and with thy whole strength."